THIRD EDITION

SUMMIT 1A

ENGLISH FOR TODAY'S WORLD

JOAN SASLOW
ALLEN ASCHER

Summit: English for Today's World Level 1A, Third Edition

Pearson, 221 River Street, Hoboken, NJ 07030

Staff credits: The people who made up the *Summit* team representing editorial, production, design, manufacturing, and marketing are Pietro Alongi, Rhea Banker, Peter Benson, Stephanie Bullard, Jennifer Castro, Tracey Munz Cataldo, Rosa Chapinal, Aerin Csigay, Dave Dickey, Gina DiLillo, Christopher Leonowicz, Laurie Neaman, Alison Pei, Sherri Pemberton, Jennifer Raspiller, Mary Rich, Courtney Steers, Katherine Sullivan, and Paula Van Ells.

Cover credit: Tonis Pan/Shutterstock

Text composition: emc design ltd

Library of Congress Cataloging-in-Publication Data

Names: Saslow, Joan M., author. | Ascher, Allen, author.
Title: Summit : English for today's world / Joan Saslow and Allen Ascher.
Description: Third Edition. | White Plains, NY : Pearson Education, [2017]
Identifiers: LCCN 2016017942| ISBN 9780134096070 (book w/ CD) | ISBN
    9780134176888 (book w/ CD) | ISBN 013409607X (book w/ CD)
Subjects: LCSH: English language--Textbooks for foreign speakers. | English
    language--Rhetoric. | English language--Sound recording for foreign
    speakers.
Classification: LCC PE1128 .S2757 2017 | DDC 428.2/4--dc23
LC record available at https://lccn.loc.gov/2016017942

Photo credits: Original photography by Libby Ballengee/MPS. Page 2 Trevor Clifford/Pearson Education; p. 3 Jenner/Fotolia; p. 4 (top left to right) Ammentorp/Fotolia, Fotos593/Shutterstock, Mark Bowden/Getty Images, Claudia Paulussen/Fotolia, (bottom left to right) Viorel Sima/Shutterstock, Avava/Fotolia, DragonImages/Fotolia, Antonioguillem/Fotolia; p. 5 CP Cheah/Moment Open/Getty Images; p. 6 (tl) Tatyana Gladskih/Fotolia, (tr) Asife/Fotolia, (bl) michael spring/Fotolia, (br) Minerva Studio/Fotolia; p. 10 Kris Yeager/Shutterstock; p. 11 Nik_Merkulov/Fotolia; p. 14 (tr) Blend Images/KidStock/Getty Images, (mr) Kevin Dodge/Blend Images/Getty Images, (br) Brian A Jackson/Shutterstock, (bottom) DJ/AAD/starmaxinc.com/Newscom; p. 16 (tl) Philip Date/Fotolia, (r) Monkey Business Images/Shutterstock, (bl) nyul/Fotolia, p. 17 V&P Photo Studio/Fotolia; p. 18 (girl) Deposit Photos/Glow Images, (background) karandaev/Fotolia; p. 19 Astarot/Fotolia; p. 20 (bl) Alexander Tihonov/Shutterstock; p. 21 (gears) ShpilbergStudios/Fotolia, (l) RSD/APC/ZOJ WENN Photos/Newscom, (c) DESRUS BENEDICTE/SIPA/Newscom, (r) Graham Whitby Boot/Allstar/Sportsphoto Ltd./Allstar/Newscom; p. 22 (tl) EDHAR/Shutterstock, (tc) rasstock/Fotolia, (tr) aastock/Shutterstock, (bl) Mike Goldwater/Alamy Stock Photo, (br) TommL/Vetta/Getty Images; p. 23 Lance Iversen/San Francisco Chronicle/Corbis; p. 27 Fancy Collection/Superstock; p. 29 Vereshchagin Dmitry/Shutterstock; p. 30 (tl) Blvdone/Fotolia, (r) nyul/Fotolia, (b) vadymvdrobot/Fotolia; p. 31 Karen Roach/Fotolia; p. 33 photobuay/Fotolia; p. 34 Doctors Without Borders, Coral Reef Alliance, (l) dpa picture alliance/Alamy Stock Photo, (r) Vlad61/Shutterstock; p. 35 ballabeyla/Fotolia; p. 38 (left to right) Raisa Kanareva/Fotolia, Olga Bogatyrenko/Shutterstock, Maridav/Fotolia, leungchopan/Fotolia, mimagephotography/Shutterstock, Sundikova/Fotolia; p. 41 (left to right) DRB Images, LLC/E+/Getty Images, Vlad Teodor/Shutterstock, Andrey Kiselev/Fotolia, Andrey Kiselev/Fotolia, Jenner/Fotolia, (b) djoronimo/Fotolia; p. 42 (l) Gstockstudio/Fotolia, (c) Matthew Cole/Shutterstock, (r) michaeljung/Fotolia; p. 44 Meffista/Fotolia; p. 45 (l) RUNGROJ YONGRIT/Newscom, (c) Valua Vitaly/Shutterstock, (r) Pearson Education; p. 46 Imagine China/Newscom; p. 47 Zdenka Darula/Fotolia; p. 50 (l) anzemulec/Fotolia, (r) Photodisc/Fotolia; p. 51 Stock Rocket/Shutterstock, (inset) maron/Fotolia; p. 55 Deyan Georgiev/Fotolia; p. 56 davidf/E+/Getty Images; p. 58 (inset) INB/Ivan Nikolov/WENN/Newscom, (bottom) Savostyanov/ZUMA Press/Newscom; p. 59 (left to right) Jerry Sharp/Shutterstock, FiCo74/Fotolia, kalpis/Fotolia; p. 60 icsnaps/Fotolia; p. 61 wavebreakmedia/Shutterstock.

Illustration credits: Aptara pp. 9, 40(b); Steve Attoe p. 52; Dusan Petricic p. 28; Shannon Wheelie p. 32.

Printed in the United States of America

ISBN-10: 0-13-449899-2
ISBN-13: 978-0-13-449899-7
1 17

pearsonelt.com/summit3e

ABOUT THE AUTHORS

Joan Saslow

Joan Saslow has taught in a variety of programs in South America and the United States. She is author or coauthor of a number of widely used courses, some of which are *Ready to Go*, *Workplace Plus*, *Literacy Plus*, and *Top Notch*. She is also author of *English in Context*, a series for reading science and technology. Ms. Saslow was the series director of *True Colors* and *True Voices*. She has participated in the English Language Specialist Program in the U.S. Department of State's Bureau of Educational and Cultural Affairs.

Allen Ascher

Allen Ascher has been a teacher and teacher trainer in China and the United States, as well as academic director of the intensive English program at Hunter College. Mr. Ascher has also been an ELT publisher and was responsible for publication and expansion of numerous well-known courses including *True Colors*, *NorthStar*, the *Longman TOEFL Preparation Series*, and the *Longman Academic Writing Series*. He is coauthor of *Top Notch*, and he wrote the "Teaching Speaking" module of *Teacher Development Interactive*, an online multimedia teacher-training program.

Ms. Saslow and Mr. Ascher are frequent presenters at professional conferences and have been coauthoring courses for teens, adults, and young adults since 2002.

AUTHORS' ACKNOWLEDGMENTS

The authors wish to thank Katherine Klagsbrun for developing the digital Extra Challenge Reading Activities that appear with all reading selections in *Summit 1*.

The authors are indebted to these reviewers, who provided extensive and detailed feedback and suggestions for *Summit*, as well as the hundreds of teachers who completed surveys and participated in focus groups.

Cris Asperti, CEL LEP, São Paulo, Brazil • **Diana Alicia Ávila Martínez**, CUEC, Monterrey, Mexico • **Shannon Brown**, Nagoya University of Foreign Studies, Nagoya, Japan • **Cesar Byrd**, Universidad ETAC Campus Chalco, Mexico City, Mexico • **Maria Claudia Campos de Freitas**, Metalanguage, São Paulo, Brazil • **Alvaro Del Castillo Alba**, CBA, Santa Cruz, Bolivia • **Isidro Castro Galván**, Instituto Teocalli, Monterrey, Mexico • **Melisa Celi**, Idiomas Católica, Lima, Peru • **Carlos Celis**, CEL LEP, São Paulo, Brazil • **Jussara Costa e Silva**, Prize Language School, São Paulo, Brazil • **Inara Couto**, CEL LEP, São Paulo, Brazil • **Gemma Crouch**, ICPNA Chiclayo, Peru • **Ingrid Valverde Diaz del Olmo**, ICPNA Cusco, Peru • **Jacqueline Díaz Esquivel**, PROULEX, Guadalajara, Mexico • **María Eid Ceneviva**, CBA, Cochabamba, Bolivia • **Erika Licia Esteves Silva**, Murphy English, São Paulo, Brazil • **Cristian Garay**, Idiomas Católica, Lima, Peru • **Miguel Angel Guerrero Pozos**, PROULEX, Guadalajara, Mexico • **Anderson Francisco Guimarães Maia**, Centro Cultural Brasil Estados Unidos, Belém, Brazil • **Cesar Guzmán**, CAADI Monterrey, Mexico • **César Iván Hernández Escobedo**, PROULEX, Guadalajara, Mexico • **Robert Hinton**, Nihon University, Tokyo, Japan • **Segundo Huanambal Díaz**, ICPNA Chiclayo, Peru • **Chandra Víctor Jacobs Sukahai**, Universidad de Valle de México, Monterrey, Mexico • **Yeni Jiménez Torres**, Centro Colombo Americano Bogotá, Colombia • **Simon Lees**, Nagoya University of Foreign Studies, Japan • **Thomas LeViness**, PROULEX, Guadalajara, Mexico • **Amy Lewis**, Waseda University, Tokyo, Japan • **Luz Libia Rey**, Centro Colombo Americano, Bogotá, Colombia • **Diego López**, Idiomas Católica, Lima, Peru • **Junior Lozano**, Idiomas Católica, Lima, Peru • **Tanja McCandie**, Nanzan University, Nagoya, Japan • **Tammy Martínez Nieves**, Universidad Autónoma de Nuevo León, Monterrey, Mexico • **María Teresa Meléndez Mantilla**, ICPNA Chiclayo, Peru • **Mónica Nomberto**, ICPNA Chiclayo, Peru • **Otilia Ojeda**, Monterrey, Mexico • **Juana Palacios**, Idiomas Católica, Lima, Peru • **Giuseppe Paldino Mayorga**, Jellyfish Learning Center, San Cristobal, Ecuador • **Henry Eduardo Pardo Lamprea**, Universidad Militar Nueva Granada, Colombia • **Dario Paredes**, Centro Colombo Americano, Bogotá, Colombia • **Teresa Noemí Parra Alarcón**, Centro Anglo Americano de Cuernavaca, S.C., Cuernavaca, Mexico • **Carlos Eduardo de la Paz Arroyo**, Centro Anglo Americano de Cuernavaca, S.C., Cuernavaca, Mexico • **José Luis Pérez Treviño**, Instituto Obispado, Monterrey, Mexico • **Evelize Maria Plácido Florian**, São Paulo, Brazil • **Armida Rivas**, Monterrey, Mexico • **Luis Rodríguez Amau**, ICPNA Chiclayo, Peru • **Fabio Ossaamn Rok Kaku**, Prize Language School, São Paulo, Brazil • **Ana María Román Villareal**, CUEC, Monterrey, Mexico • **Reynaldo Romano C.**, CBA, La Paz, Bolivia • **Francisco Rondón**, Centro Colombo Americano, Bogotá, Colombia • **Peter Russell**, Waseda University, Tokyo, Japan • **Rubena St. Louis**, Universidad Simón Bolivar, Caracas, Venezuela • **Marisol Salazar**, Centro Colombo Americano, Bogotá, Colombia • **Miguel Sierra**, Idiomas Católica, Lima, Peru • **Greg Strong**, Aoyama Gakuin University, Tokyo, Japan • **Gerald Talandis**, Toyama University, Toyama, Japan • **Stephen Thompson**, Nagoya University of Foreign Studies, Nagoya, Japan • **José Luis Urbina Hurtado**, Instituto Tecnológico de León, Mexico • **René F. Valdivia Pereyra**, CBA, Santa Cruz, Bolivia • **Magno Alejandro Vivar Hurtado**, Salesian Polytechnic University, Ecuador • **Belkis Yanes**, Caracas, Venezuela • **Holger Zamora**, ICPNA Cusco, Peru • **Maria Cristina Zanon Costa**, Metalanguage, São Paulo, Brazil • **Kathia Zegarra**, Idiomas Católica, Lima, Peru.

LEARNING OBJECTIVES

UNIT	COMMUNICATION GOALS	VOCABULARY	GRAMMAR
UNIT 1 **Outlook and Behavior** PAGE 2	• Describe your personality • Discuss someone's behavior • Compare perspectives on world problems • Discuss creative ways to achieve a goal	• Adjectives to describe personality traits **Word Study:** • Adjective suffixes -ful and -less	• Gerunds and infinitives: review and expansion • Verbs that require a noun or pronoun before an infinitive **GRAMMAR BOOSTER** • Infinitives: review, expansion, and common errors • Grammar for writing: parallelism with gerunds and infinitives
UNIT 2 **Music and Other Arts** PAGE 14	• Describe how you've been enjoying the arts • Express a negative opinion politely • Describe a creative personality • Discuss the benefits of the arts	• Elements of music • Negative descriptions of music • Describing creative personalities **Word Study:** • Using participial adjectives	• The present perfect continuous • Cleft sentences with <u>What</u> **GRAMMAR BOOSTER** • Finished and unfinished actions: summary • Noun clauses: review and expansion • Grammar for Writing: noun clauses as adjective and noun complements
UNIT 3 **Money, Finance, and You** PAGE 26	• Express buyer's remorse • Talk about financial goals and plans • Discuss good and bad money management • Explain reasons for charitable giving	• Describing spending styles • Expressing buyer's remorse • Good and bad money management **Word Study:** • Parts of speech	• Expressing regrets about the past: <u>wish</u> + past perfect; <u>should have</u> / <u>ought to have</u> + past participle; <u>if only</u> + past perfect. • Completed future actions and plans: The future perfect and perfect infinitives **GRAMMAR BOOSTER** • The past unreal conditional: inverted form • The future continuous • The future perfect continuous
UNIT 4 **Clothing and Appearance** PAGE 38	• Describe clothing details and formality • Talk about changes in clothing customs • Examine questionable cosmetic procedures • Discuss appearance and self-esteem	• Adjectives to describe fashion • Describing clothes **Word Study:** • Compound words with <u>self-</u>	• Quantifiers: review and expansion **GRAMMAR BOOSTER** • <u>A few</u> / <u>few</u>; <u>a little</u> / <u>little</u> • Quantifiers: using <u>of</u> for specific reference • Quantifiers used without referents • Grammar for Writing: subject-verb agreement of quantifiers followed by <u>of</u>
UNIT 5 **Communities** PAGE 50	• Politely ask someone not to do something • Complain about public conduct • Suggest ways to avoid being a victim of urban crime • Discuss the meaning of community	• Types of locations • Community service activities **Word Study:** • Using negative prefixes to form antonyms	• Possessive gerunds • Paired conjunctions **GRAMMAR BOOSTER** • Conjunctions with <u>so</u>, <u>too</u>, <u>neither</u>, or <u>not either</u> • <u>So</u>, <u>too</u>, <u>neither</u>, or <u>not either</u>: short responses

CONVERSATION STRATEGIES	LISTENING / PRONUNCIATION	READING	WRITING
• Use <u>I'd say</u> to soften an assertive opinion • Use <u>I don't see [myself] that way</u> to politely contradict another's statement • Say <u>I see [you] as</u> to explain your own point of view • Use <u>tend to</u> and <u>seem to</u> to make generalizations	• Listen to activate grammar • Listen to classify • Listen for main ideas • Listen for details • Understand meaning from context **PRONUNCIATION BOOSTER** • Content words and function words	**Texts:** • A survey about positive and negative outlooks • Descriptions of other people's behavior • A newspaper article about a creative solution to a problem **Skills / strategies:** • Understand idioms and expressions • Determine the main idea • Understand meaning from context • Summarize	**Task:** • Write about your outlook on a world problem **Skill:** • Paragraph structure: Review
• Use <u>To tell the truth</u>, <u>To be honest</u>, and <u>I hate to say it, but</u> to politely introduce a contrary opinion	• Listen to activate vocabulary • Listen for main ideas • Listen for supporting information • Listen to take notes • Listen for details **PRONUNCIATION BOOSTER** • Intonation patterns	**Texts:** • A survey about musical memories • Commentaries about enjoying the arts • A short biography **Skills / strategies:** • Understand idioms and expressions • Infer information • Identify supporting details • Express and support an opinion	**Task:** • Describe your interests and personality **Skill:** • Parallel structure
• Use <u>You know, ...</u> to introduce a new topic of conversation • Use <u>I hate to say it, but</u> to introduce negative information • Ask <u>What do you mean?</u> to invite someone to elaborate • Say <u>That's a shame</u> to show empathy • Say <u>I'll think about that</u> when you're non-committal about someone's suggestion	• Listen for details • Listen to activate vocabulary • Listen to confirm content • Listen to summarize • Listen to evaluate **PRONUNCIATION BOOSTER** • Sentence rhythm: thought groups	**Texts:** • A spending habits self-test • Interview responses about financial goals • A guide to charitable giving **Skills / strategies:** • Understand idioms and expressions • Understand meaning from context • Draw conclusions • Express and support an opinion	**Task:** • Write a personal statement about how you manage financial responsibilities **Skill:** • Organizing information by degrees of importance
• Use <u>Can I ask you a question about...?</u> to introduce a subject you are unsure of • Use <u>I mean</u> to elaborate on a prior statement or question • Use <u>Actually,</u> to assert a point of view • Begin a question with <u>So</u> to affirm understanding of someone's earlier statement • Say <u>I think that might be ...</u> to gently warn that something is inappropriate	• Listen for main ideas • Listen for details • Listen to summarize **PRONUNCIATION BOOSTER** • Linking sounds	**Texts:** • Descriptions of personal style • An article about the evolution of "business casual" attire • An article about questionable cosmetic procedures • Advertisements for cosmetic procedures **Skills / strategies:** • Understand idioms and expressions • Understand meaning from context • Identify supporting details • Express and support an opinion	**Task:** • Write two paragraphs comparing tastes in fashion **Skill:** • Compare and contrast: Review
• Use <u>Do you mind...?</u> to ask permission to do something • Use <u>Not at all</u> to affirm that you are not bothered or inconvenienced • Use <u>That's very [considerate] of you</u> to thank someone for accommodating you	• Listen to summarize • Listen for details • Listen to confirm content • Listen to infer **PRONUNCIATION BOOSTER** • Unstressed syllables: vowel reduction to /ə/	**Texts:** • A questionnaire about community • Interview responses about pet peeves • A magazine article about urban crime • A website about community projects **Skills / strategies:** • Understand idioms and expressions • Classify • Understand meaning from context • Critical thinking	**Task:** • Write a formal letter of complaint **Skill:** • Formal letters: Review

UNIT	COMMUNICATION GOALS	VOCABULARY	GRAMMAR
UNIT 6 **Animals** PAGE 62	• Exchange opinions about the treatment of animals • Discuss the pros and cons of certain pets • Compare animal and human behavior • Debate the value of animal conservation	• Categories of animals • Describing pets • Animal social groups and physical features	• Passive modals **GRAMMAR BOOSTER** • Modals and modal-like expressions: summary
UNIT 7 **Advertising and Consumers** PAGE 74	• Evaluate ways and places to shop • Discuss your reactions to ads • Discuss problem shopping behavior • Persuade someone to buy a product	• Verbs for shopping activities • Ways to persuade	• Passive forms of gerunds and infinitives **GRAMMAR BOOSTER** • The passive voice: review and expansion
UNIT 8 **Family Trends** PAGE 86	• Describe family trends • Discuss parent-teen issues • Compare generations • Discuss caring for the elderly	• Describing parent and teen behavior **Word Study:** • Transforming verbs and adjectives into nouns	• Repeated comparatives and double comparatives **GRAMMAR BOOSTER** • Making comparisons: review and expansion • Other uses of comparatives, superlatives, and comparisons with <u>as...as</u>
UNIT 9 **Facts, Theories, and Hoaxes** PAGE 98	• Speculate about everyday situations • Present a theory • Discuss how believable a story is • Evaluate the trustworthiness of news sources	• Degrees of certainty **Word Study:** • Adjectives with the suffix <u>-able</u>	• Perfect modals for speculating about the past: active and passive voice **GRAMMAR BOOSTER** • Perfect modals: short responses (active and passive voice)
UNIT 10 **Your Free Time** PAGE 110	• Suggest ways to reduce stress • Describe how you got interested in a hobby • Discuss how mobile devices affect us • Compare attitudes about taking risks	• Ways to describe people • Ways to reduce stress **Word Study:** • Adverbs of manner	• Expressing an expectation with <u>be supposed to</u> • Describing past repeated or habitual actions: <u>would</u> and the past continuous with <u>always</u> **GRAMMAR BOOSTER** • <u>Be supposed to</u>: expansion • <u>Would</u>: review • Grammar for Writing: placement of adverbs of manner

Reference Charts . . . . page 122
Grammar Booster . . . . page 125
Pronunciation Booster . . . . page 141
Test-Taking Skills Booster . . . . page 151

CONVERSATION STRATEGIES	LISTENING / PRONUNCIATION	READING	WRITING
• Use <u>I've heard</u> to introduce a commonly-held belief or opinion • Respond with <u>In what way?</u> to request further explanation • Use <u>For one thing</u> to introduce a first supporting argument • Use <u>And besides</u> to add another supporting argument • Use <u>But what if</u> to suggest a hypothetical situation	• Listen to activate vocabulary • Listen to define terms • Listen for examples • Listen for details **PRONUNCIATION BOOSTER** • Sound reduction	**Texts:** • Social media posts about treatment of animals • An article about animal conservation **Skills / strategies:** • Understand idioms and expressions • Understand meaning from context • Recognize cause and effect	**Task:** • Write a persuasive essay about the treatment of animals **Skill:** • Supporting a point of view
• Say <u>Quick question</u> to indicate one wants some simple information • Introduce an opinion with <u>I find</u> • Say <u>That's good to know</u> to express satisfaction for information • Use <u>Why don't you…</u> to offer advice	• Listen to activate vocabulary • Listen to infer **PRONUNCIATION BOOSTER** • Vowel sounds /i/ and /ɪ/	**Texts:** • Self-tests about shopping mistakes and behavior • Descriptions of techniques used in advertising • Interview responses about compulsive shopping **Skills / strategies:** • Understand idioms and expressions • Understand meaning from context • Identify supporting details	**Task:** • Write a summary of an article **Skill:** • Summarize and paraphrase someone's point of view
• Ask <u>Why's that?</u> to ask someone to elaborate on an opinion • Say <u>I suppose, but …</u> to signal partial agreement	• Listen to activate grammar • Listen to activate vocabulary • Listen for supporting information • Listen for details • Listen to compare and contrast **PRONUNCIATION BOOSTER** • Stress placement: prefixes and suffixes	**Texts:** • A survey about parents and teens • A brochure about falling birthrates • A report on the increase in global population of older people **Skills / strategies:** • Understand idioms and expressions • Summarize • Understand meaning from context • Critical thinking • Draw conclusions	**Task:** • Write a blog post of three or more paragraphs about advice for parents and teens **Skill:** • Avoiding run-on sentences and comma splices
• Use <u>I wonder</u> to introduce something you're not sure about • Say <u>I'm sure it's nothing</u> to indicate that something is probably not serious • Say <u>I suppose you're right</u> to acknowledge someone's point of view • Say <u>There must be a good explanation</u> to assure someone that things will turn out OK	• Listen to activate vocabulary • Listen for main ideas • Listen to draw conclusions **PRONUNCIATION BOOSTER** • Reduction and linking in perfect modals in the passive voice	**Texts:** • A quiz about tricky facts • An article about Rapa Nui • Facts and theories about mysteries • An article about a UFO conspiracy theory • A survey about the trustworthiness of information sources **Skills / strategies:** • Understand idioms and expressions • Confirm point of view • Infer information	**Task:** • Write a news article about a mysterious event **Skill:** • Avoiding sentence fragments
• Say <u>Uh-oh</u> to indicate that you realize you've made a mistake • Use <u>I just realized</u> to acknowledge a mistake • Use <u>Well, frankly</u> to indicate that you are going to be honest about something • Use <u>It's just that</u> or <u>Let's face it</u> to introduce an honest criticism or assessment • Use <u>You know what?</u> to introduce a piece of advice	• Listen to activate vocabulary • Listen for main ideas • Listen for supporting details • Listen to understand meaning from context **PRONUNCIATION BOOSTER** • Vowel sounds /eɪ/, /ɛ/, /æ/, and /ʌ/	**Texts:** • A survey about free time • Descriptions of how people got interested in their hobbies • An article about the impact of mobile devices • A survey about mobile device usage **Skills / strategies:** • Understand idioms and expressions • Understand meaning from context • Identify supporting details • Infer point of view	**Task:** • Write a critique of an article **Skill:** • Presenting and supporting opinions clearly

What is *Summit?*

Summit is a two-level high-intermediate to advanced communicative course that develops confident, culturally fluent English speakers able to navigate the social, travel, and professional situations they will encounter as they use English in their lives. *Summit* can follow the intermediate level of any communicative series, including the four-level *Top Notch* course.

Summit delivers immediate, demonstrable results in every class session through its proven pedagogy and systematic and intensive recycling of language. Each goal- and achievement-based lesson is tightly correlated to the Can-Do Statements of the Common European Framework of Reference (CEFR). The course is fully benchmarked to the Global Scale of English (GSE).

Each level of *Summit* contains material for 60 to 90 hours of classroom instruction. Its full array of additional print and digital components can extend instruction to 120 hours if desired. Furthermore, the entire *Summit* course can be tailored to blended learning with its integrated online component, *MyEnglishLab*. *Summit* offers more ready-to-use teacher resources than any other course available today.

NEW This third edition represents a major revision of content and has a greatly increased quantity of exercises, both print and digital. Following are some key new features:

- **Conversation Activator Videos** to build communicative competence
- **Discussion Activator Videos** to increase quality and quantity of expression
- A **Test-Taking Skills Booster** (and **Extra Challenge Reading Activities**) to help students succeed in the reading and listening sections of standardized tests
- An **Understand Idioms and Expressions** section in each unit increases the authenticity of student spoken language

Award-Winning Instructional Design*

Demonstrable confirmation of progress

Every two-page lesson has a clearly stated communication goal and culminates in a guided conversation, free discussion, debate, presentation, role play, or project that achieves the goal. Idea framing and notepadding activities lead students to confident spoken expression.

Cultural fluency

Summit audio familiarizes students with a wide variety of native and non-native accents. Discussion activities reflect the topics people of diverse cultural backgrounds talk about in their social and professional lives.

Explicit vocabulary and grammar

Clear captioned illustrations and dictionary-style presentations, all with audio, take the guesswork out of meaning and ensure comprehensible pronunciation. Grammar is embedded in context and presented explicitly for form, meaning, and use. The unique "Recycle this Language" feature encourages active use of newly learned words and grammar during communication practice.

Active listening syllabus

More than 50 listening tasks at each level of *Summit* develop critical thinking and crucial listening comprehension skills such as listen for details, main ideas, confirmation of content, inference, and understand meaning from context.

Summit is the recipient of the Association of Educational Publishers'
Distinguished Achievement Award.

Conversation and Discussion Activators

Memorable conversation models with audio provide appealing natural social language and conversation strategies essential for post-secondary learners. Rigorous Conversation Activator and Discussion Activator activities with video systematically stimulate recycling of social language, ensuring it is not forgotten. A unique Pronunciation Booster provides lessons and interactive practice, with audio, so students can improve their spoken expression.

Systematic writing skills development

Summit teaches the conventions of correct English writing so students will be prepared for standardized tests, academic study, and professional communication. Lessons cover key writing and rhetorical skills such as using parallel structure and avoiding sentence fragments, run-on sentences, and comma splices. Intensive work in paragraph and essay development ensures confident and successful writing.

Reading skills and strategies

Each unit of *Summit* builds critical thinking and key reading skills and strategies such as paraphrasing, drawing conclusions, expressing and supporting an opinion, and activating prior knowledge. Learners develop analytical skills and increase fluency while supporting their answers through speaking.

*We wish you and your students enjoyment and success with **Summit**. We wrote it for you.*
Joan Saslow and Allen Ascher

ActiveTeach

Maximize the impact of your *Summit* lessons. Digital Student's Book pages with access to all audio and video provide an interactive classroom experience that can be used with or without an interactive whiteboard (IWB). It includes a full array of easy-to-access digital and printable features.

For class presentation . . .

 NEW Conversation Activator videos: increase students' confidence in oral communication

 NEW Discussion Activator videos: increase quality and quantity of expression

 NEW Extra Grammar Exercises: ensure mastery of grammar

 NEW Extra Challenge Reading Activities: help students succeed at standardized proficiency tests.

PLUS

- Interactive Whiteboard tools, including zoom, highlight, links, notes, and more.
- ▶ Clickable Audio: instant access to the complete classroom audio program
- *Summit TV* Video Program: fully-revised authentic TV documentaries as well as unscripted on-the-street interviews, featuring a variety of regional and non-native accents

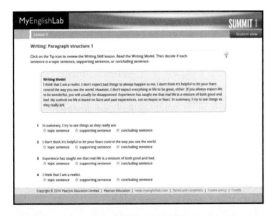

For planning . . .

- A *Methods Handbook* for a communicative classroom
- Detailed timed lesson plans for each two-page lesson
- *Summit TV* teaching notes
- Complete answer keys, audio scripts, and video scripts

For extra support . . .

- Hundreds of extra printable activities, with teaching notes
- *Summit TV* activity worksheets

For assessment . . .

- Ready-made unit and review achievement tests with options to edit, add, or delete items.

Ready-made Summit Web Projects provide authentic application of lesson language.

MyEnglishLab

An optional online learning tool

- **NEW** Immediate, meaningful feedback on wrong answers
- **NEW** Remedial grammar exercises
- **NEW** Grammar Coach videos for general reference
- Interactive practice of all material presented in the course
- Grade reports that display performance and time on task
- Auto-graded achievement tests

Workbook

Lesson-by-lesson written exercises to accompany the Student's Book

Full-Course Placement Tests

Choose printable or online version

Classroom Audio Program

- A set of Audio CDs, as an alternative to the clickable audio in ActiveTeach
- Contains a variety of authentic regional and non-native accents to build comprehension of diverse English speakers
- **NEW** The app *Summit Go* allows access anytime, anywhere and lets students practice at their own pace. The entire audio program is also available for students at www.english.com/summit3e.

Teacher's Edition and Lesson Planner

- Detailed interleaved lesson plans, language and culture notes, answer keys, and more
- Also accessible in digital form in ActiveTeach

For more information: www.pearsonelt.com/summit3e

PREVIEW

A **FRAME YOUR IDEAS**   Complete the quiz by writing your points in the circles. Then calculate your score.

QUIZ

Optimist, Realist, or Pessimist?

"Is the glass half full or half empty?"

How do you see the world? Do you have a positive or a negative outlook?

1
○ You wake up in the middle of the night with a stomachache. Your first thought is...

"I'm sure it's nothing. I'll just go back to sleep."
1 point

"It's probably nothing serious. I'll just take some medicine."
2 points

"This could be serious. I'd better go to the doctor."
3 points

2
○ You apply for your "dream job," but you don't get it. You think...

"I guess this wasn't really my dream job. I'll find a better job somewhere else."
1 point

"Oh, well. You win some and you lose some."
2 points

"I'll never get the job I want."
3 points

3
○ When you are introduced to someone new, you...

assume that person is a nice person.
1 point

keep an open mind about whether you'll like each other.
2 points

assume that person won't like or respect you.
3 points

4
○ If someone unexpectedly knocks on your door, you think...

"Great! It's probably a friend or a relative here to surprise me."
1 point

"I wonder who that could be. I'll go find out."
2 points

"I'm not answering. It could be a salesperson or even a criminal."
3 points

5
○ Your boss invites you to have lunch in a restaurant. You say to yourself...

"I must be getting a promotion or a raise. That's really nice!"
1 point

"My boss must like to socialize with everyone from time to time."
2 points

"Uh-oh! There must be some problem with my work."
3 points

6
○ News about crime or disasters makes you...

think about how you can help.
1 point

realize that sometimes bad things happen.
2 points

feel very unsafe.
3 points

ADD UP YOUR POINTS

6–9 POINTS
You're an optimist.
You have a positive outlook and tend to see the glass half full.

10–14 POINTS
You're a realist.
You tend to see the world as it really is.

15–18 POINTS
You're a pessimist.
You have a negative outlook and tend to see the glass half empty.

B **PAIR WORK**   Compare answers with a partner. Are your scores similar, or very different? Which of you has the more optimistic, realistic, or pessimistic outlook on life, according to the quiz?

C **GROUP WORK**   Calculate the average score for the members of the class. On average, how optimistic, realistic, or pessimistic is your class?

D ▶ 1:02 **SPOTLIGHT**   Read and listen to two friends talking about a new virus they're concerned about. Notice the spotlighted language.

Leo: Did you hear about that new virus going around? Chikungunya?
Nora: Chikun-*what*? Oh! You mean the one that comes from mosquitos?
Leo: As a matter of fact, yes. Just like Zika.
Nora: We've never had either of those viruses here before.
Leo: Well, they say it's due to global warming — all those mosquitos from the warmer weather. I suppose **it's just a matter of time** 'til we get all kinds of new diseases.
Nora: You sure are a pessimist. I agree it's scary. But hey, **what are you going to do?**
Leo: I'm just saying this **has started getting to me** and I'm scared. I read that if you come down with Chikungunya, you can be sick for a year … or even more.
Nora: Right. But they say it's still pretty rare around here. These things are just part of life. **You've got to roll with the punches**, if you know what I mean. I'm not going to worry about it.
Leo: Well, *I* am. Anyway, I'm not going to the company dinner at that outdoor restaurant. **You're just a sitting duck** out there, with the mosquitos and everything.
Nora: What about just wearing long sleeves and hoping for the best? I mean, how unlucky could you be?
Leo: Well, I'm going to call in sick and say I can't go. **Better safe than sorry**.

E **UNDERSTAND IDIOMS AND EXPRESSIONS**   Find the following expressions in Spotlight. Choose the meaning that more closely explains each one.

1 It's just a matter of time.
   a It will take a long time.
   b It will certainly happen in the future.

2 Hey, what are you going to do?
   a There's nothing anyone can do about it.
   b What plans do you have?

3 This has started getting to me.
   a This is beginning to bother me.
   b I'm beginning to get sick.

4 You've got to roll with the punches.
   a You have to deal with life's difficulties and move on.
   b You shouldn't accept the difficulties life brings.

5 You're just a sitting duck out there.
   a There's nothing you can do to protect yourself.
   b You probably won't get sick.

6 Better safe than sorry.
   a It's better to stay safe and have no regrets.
   b I'm sorry, but I'm sick.

F **COMPARE AND CONTRAST**   Discuss the questions.

1 How would you describe Leo's and Nora's outlooks? How are they different?

2 Who are you more like, Leo or Nora?

SPEAKING **ROLE PLAY**   Take turns responding to the following statements related to the situations in the quiz on page 2. Use idioms from Exercise E in your responses. Then change roles.

❝I woke up with a stomachache. This could be serious. I'd better go to the doctor.❞

❝I'll never get the job I want!❞

❝My boss invited me to lunch in a restaurant. There must be some problem with my work.❞

❝Uh-oh. There's someone at the door. I'm not answering. It could be a salesperson or even a criminal.❞

3

DIGITAL STRATEGIES

A ▶ 1:03 **VOCABULARY** ADJECTIVES TO DESCRIBE PERSONALITY TRAITS

Read and listen. Then listen again and repeat.

Nothing seems to bother Donna. She just rolls with the punches.

She's pretty **easygoing**.

Jason never wastes time at work and always gets a lot done.

He's quite **hardworking**.

Andrés is always helpful. He's aware of other people's needs.

He's really **considerate**.

Sonia's a tennis champion, but she doesn't think she's better than anyone else.

She's quite **modest**.

Eric is not at all shy. He loves meeting and chatting with new people.

He's so **outgoing**.

You can trust Irene to be reliable. She always does a good job and finishes it on time.

She's very **trustworthy**.

Jared rarely acts silly. He is thoughtful and pays attention to the important things.

He's pretty **serious**.

Isabelle and Anna enjoy chatting with each other.

They're really **talkative**.

B **CLASSIFY THE VOCABULARY** On the chart, classify the adjectives from the Vocabulary, and other adjectives you know, according to your opinion. Then discuss with a partner.

Are always positive   Can be either   Are always negative

> 66 Hardworking is usually positive. But some people are too hardworking and don't spend enough time with their family. 99

Other adjectives
polite
impolite
punctual
rude
friendly
unfriendly
nice
liberal
conservative
interesting
intelligent
independent

 DIGITAL INDUCTIVE ACTIVITY

C **GRAMMAR** GERUNDS AND INFINITIVES: REVIEW AND EXPANSION

Remember: Gerunds and infinitives function as subjects, objects, and subject complements in sentences.

Subject: Sharing tasks with co-workers is helpful.
Direct object of a verb: I avoid **calling** the doctor too often.
Subject complement: Our dream is **to make** a trip to Africa next year.

Some verbs can only be followed by gerunds as the object of the verb. Some verbs can only be followed by infinitives. Others can be followed by either a gerund or an infinitive.

We **considered going** to the picnic. NOT We considered to go to the picnic.
They **have decided to invite** their teacher to the play. NOT They have decided inviting their teacher to the play.
BUT
She **prefers going** to the early show. OR She **prefers to go** to the early show.

For lists of verbs followed by gerunds and / or infinitives, see pages 123–124.

For a list of expressions followed by gerunds, see page 123.

For a list of adjectives followed by infinitives, see page 124.

Prepositions can be followed by gerunds, not by infinitives.

I saw a film **about driving** across the United States.

NOT I saw a film about ~~to drive~~ across the United States.

Adjectives can be followed by infinitives, not by gerunds.

We're **ready to go.** NOT We're ready ~~going~~.

Other uses of infinitives:

To state a fact or an opinion with an impersonal <u>it</u> + an infinitive.

It's a good day **to meet** the new boss.

To state the purpose of an action.

We used an insect repellent **to avoid** mosquito bites.

To modify an adjective with <u>too</u> or <u>enough</u>. Note: <u>Enough</u> follows an adjective.

They were **too late to make** the plane to Boston, but they were **early enough to catch** the bus.

NOT ... they were ~~enough early to catch~~ the bus.

> **GRAMMAR BOOSTER** p. 125
> · Infinitives: review, expansion, and common errors
> · Parallelism with gerunds and infinitives

DIGITAL MORE EXERCISES

D ▶ 1:04 **LISTEN TO ACTIVATE GRAMMAR**   Listen to the conversations. Then complete each statement with the gerund or infinitive form of one of the verbs from List 1 and a word from List 2.

1 He's going to come home early ....

2 She's worried about .... Jack about her ....

3 He says it's too late ....

4 She doesn't mind .... in ....

5 She's apologizing for .... to him the night before.

6 He's a little down about .... work late on ....

List 1:	List 2:
paint	the bedroom
have to	Friday
tell	an office
be	rude
work	keyboard
watch	a movie

E **PAIR WORK**   Complete the questions with your own ideas, using gerunds or infinitives. Answer your partner's questions.

1 Do you avoid .... ?

2 When are you too old .... ?

3 In your family, who doesn't mind .... ?

4 Do you believe in .... ?

5 Do you object to .... ?

6 Do you think it's a good time .... ?

7 Do you ever stay up late .... ?

8 What don't you mind .... ?

NOW YOU CAN | Describe your personality

A ▶ 1:05 **CONVERSATION SPOTLIGHT**   Read and listen. Notice the spotlighted conversation strategies.

A: So how would you describe yourself?

B: Me? Well, **I'd say** I'm pretty easygoing. I don't let things get to me.

A: Easygoing? I see you as serious.

B: You think so? **I don't see** myself **that way**. In any case, can't you be both easygoing and serious?

A: I guess. And how would you describe me?

B: You? **I see you as** pretty outgoing.

A: You do? Why do you say that?

B: Because you **tend to be** talkative and you **seem to** like being with people a lot.

B ▶ 1:06 **RHYTHM AND INTONATION**   Listen again and repeat. Then practice the conversation with a partner.

DIGITAL VIDEO

DIGITAL SPEAKING BOOSTER

C **CONVERSATION ACTIVATOR**   Create a similar conversation, using the Vocabulary or other adjectives that describe your personality. Start like this: *So how would you describe yourself?* Be sure to change roles and then partners.

DON'T STOP!

• Say more about your personality.
• Ask about other people's personalities.
• Say as much as you can.

> **RECYCLE THIS LANGUAGE**
> be an optimist / a pessimist / a realist

GOAL Discuss someone's behavior

A ▶ 1:07 **GRAMMAR SPOTLIGHT** Read how these four people describe other people's behavior. Notice the spotlighted grammar.

My manager, Chris, is a real sweetheart. He **wants all of us to succeed**. And he **encourages us to learn** new skills so we can move up in the company. He's also really kind and understanding. He **permits us to work** at home when we have a sick kid. You'll never find a better boss than Chris!

Sarah Beth Linehan, 30 **Melbourne, Australia**

I share an apartment with three roommates, but one of them, Erika, is an annoying pain in the neck! First, she's a total workaholic. Between her studies and her after-school job, she's rarely here, and when she is, she just keeps working. My other two roommates and I do all the chores: shop for groceries, cook, wash the dishes, and so on. When we complain that Erika's not pulling her weight, she just **asks us to do** *her* chores because she doesn't have time! Time? It's time for her to move out!

Martina Braun, 21 **Frankfurt, Germany**

My colleague Lily at the travel agency where I work is a real people person. Most of us prefer to do everything by e-mail or online, but Lily **invites all her clients** (even the difficult ones!) **to come in** to the office and **tell her** their dream vacation ideas, and she tries to make those a reality for them. And Lily's such a team player. If one of us has too much to do, she offers to help. Everyone loves Lily.

Cindy Yu, 27 **Boston, USA**

I'll never forget my high-school drama teacher, Mr. Mellon. He was such a tyrant! He used to **force us to say** our lines over and over until it drove us crazy. And if anyone forgot even one word, he would **forbid them to go** home until they had learned the line. He would **warn them to learn** every line perfectly by the next class, or they couldn't be in the play. Everyone hated him. He took all the fun out of drama.

Richard Rowan, 43 **Saint Louis, USA**

B **RELATE TO PERSONAL EXPERIENCE** Find these words and phrases in the Grammar Spotlight. With a partner, talk about people you know or have known who behave like people described in the Grammar Spotlight. Provide examples.

a pain in the neck   a team player
a people person   a tyrant
a sweetheart   a workaholic

C ▶ 1:08 **LISTEN TO CLASSIFY** Listen to people describe other people's behavior, using noun and pronoun objects before infinitives. Check the description(s) of each person, according to the opinions expressed.

1 Margaret is: ☐ a workaholic   ☐ a pain in the neck   ☐ a team player
2 Peter is: ☐ a people person   ☐ a tyrant   ☐ a pain in the neck
3 Tim is: ☐ a tyrant   ☐ a pain in the neck   ☐ a workaholic

D **GRAMMAR** **VERBS THAT REQUIRE A NOUN OR PRONOUN BEFORE AN INFINITIVE**
Remember: Some verbs can be followed directly by an infinitive. However, in the active voice, some verbs must have a noun or pronoun object before the infinitive.

Active
He **ordered us to leave** the office.
The sign **warned drivers not to speed**.
We **told them to be** on time.
She **taught them to swim** last year.

Passive
(We were ordered to leave the office.)
(Drivers were warned not to speed.)
(They were told to be on time.)
(They were taught to swim last year.)

Some verbs, such as <u>would like</u>, <u>want</u>, <u>ask</u>, <u>expect</u>, and <u>need</u>, are used with or without a noun or pronoun object in the active voice, depending on the meaning.

Without an object
We'd **like to eat** healthier food.
She **wants to drive** the new car.
Tom **asked to see** the director.

With an object
We'd **like our children to eat** healthier food, too.
She **wants me to drive** the new car.
Tom **asked Emily to see** the director.

Negative infinitives
To make an infinitive negative, place <u>not</u> before the infinitive:

*They advised us **not to come** late to the meeting.*

Remember: To make a gerund negative, also place <u>not</u> before the gerund:

*They complained about **not having** enough time.*

These verbs require a noun or pronoun object before an infinitive in the active voice.

advise	convince	force	invite	permit	require
allow	encourage	hire	order	persuade	teach
cause	forbid	instruct	pay	remind	warn

For a list of verbs that can be followed directly by an infinitive in the active voice, see page 124.

E **UNDERSTAND THE GRAMMAR** On a separate sheet of paper, change each sentence to the active voice. Use the <u>by</u> phrase as the subject.

The CEO invited spouses of co-workers to attend the reception.

1 Spouses of co-workers were invited (by the CEO) to attend the reception.
2 Drivers were told (by the hotel security guards) to stop at the entrance to the hotel.
3 Employees were required (by the rules) to return from lunch at 2:00.
4 We were encouraged (by our manager) to tweet our questions to the speaker.
5 They were advised (by the invitation) to be at the restaurant before 8:00 P.M.

F **GRAMMAR PRACTICE** Complete the sentences with your own ideas, an object, and an infinitive.

1 The change in the meeting schedule caused ....*us*......... to ...*postpone our flight*... .
2 The bad weather on the day of the game convinced .... to ....
3 Should we remind .... to .... ?
4 The sign at the entrance to the event warned .... to ....
5 Why don't you pay .... to .... ?
6 The article in the newspaper about the accident persuaded .... to ....

G **PAIR WORK** With a partner, take turns answering the questions, using the cues provided.

1 **A:** Is Mark bringing the food for the picnic?
   B: No, Mark ....*expects us to bring*....... the food. (expect / us / bring)
2 **A:** Have you spoken to the manager about the broken equipment?
   B: No. I .... to her about it. (ask / Ken / speak)
3 **A:** Who's going to be the first speaker at the event?
   B: Actually, I .... the first one. (would like / you / be)
4 **A:** Do you want to write the summary of what happened at the meeting?
   B: I'd rather not. I .... it. (want / Kathy / write)
5 **B:** Didn't you need to discuss the new e-mail system with Mr. Green?
   A: Actually, I .... with him about it. (want / my assistant / speak)

PRONUNCIATION
BOOSTER   p. 141
Content words and function words

NOW YOU CAN Discuss someone's behavior

A **NOTEPADDING** Choose two people you know. Make statements about each person's personality and behavior, using one of the verbs from the list in the chart at the top of this page.

Description	Description
1	1
2	2

Description
1 My sister is a sweetheart.
She encourages everyone
to get along.

B **DISCUSSION ACTIVATOR** Discuss the people you wrote about on your notepads. Say as much as you can about them.

RECYCLE THIS
LANGUAGE
· easygoing
· hardworking
· helpful
· modest
· outgoing
· reliable
· serious
· talkative
· an optimist
· a pessimist
· a realist
· a sweetheart
· a team player

GOAL Compare perspectives on world problems

A **LISTENING WARM-UP** How much do you worry about epidemics, terrorism, and crime? Write each one on the graph. Then discuss with a partner.

NOT AT ALL ⟶ A LOT

B ▶ 1:09 **LISTEN FOR MAIN IDEAS** Listen. Write the problem discussed in each conversation.

Conversation 1 .... Conversation 2 .... Conversation 3 ....

C ▶ 1:10 **LISTEN FOR DETAILS** Listen again. Circle *T* (true), *F* (false), or *ND* (not discussed).

		T	F	ND
1	**a** She says there aren't a lot of newspaper articles about crime.	T	F	ND
	b He thinks there's nothing anyone can do about crime.	T	F	ND
2	**a** She thinks breathing the air on planes can be dangerous.	T	F	ND
	b He thinks international travel will spread the disease all over the world.	T	F	ND
3	**a** He worries about terrorism in crowded places.	T	F	ND
	b She thinks terrorism is caused by poverty.	T	F	ND

D **UNDERSTAND MEANING FROM CONTEXT** Read each quotation. Then listen again and complete each statement.

Conversation 1

1 When the woman says, "Crime is just out of control," she means ....

  a there's a huge amount of crime   **b** we have to control crime

2 When the man says, "What is the world coming to?" he is asking, ...

  a "Where in the world can we go to avoid crime?"   **b** "What is the future of the world?"

3 When he says, "Better safe than sorry," he is saying ....

  a don't tempt criminals by wearing jewelry   **b** just stay home where it's safe

Conversation 2

4 When the man says, "I think I'm getting a little obsessed," he means, ...

  a "I'm thinking about this way too much."   **b** "I'm afraid I'm getting sick."

5 When she says, "Well, I don't think that's crazy," she means ....

  a he's right to be worried   **b** the disease is extremely bad

6 When the woman says, "It's even more contagious," she worries ....

  a it could cause an epidemic   **b** it won't last for long

Conversation 3

7 When the man says, "I don't know about you, but I'm getting a little freaked out about terrorism," he's really saying, ...

  a "Are you as scared as I am about terrorism?"   **b** "I don't know how to stop terrorism. Do you?"

8 When the woman says, "Well, that's no way to live," she means, ...

  a "You are going to die."   **b** "It's impossible to live normally with that outlook."

9 When she says, "It is what it is," she means, ...

  a "What is it?"   **b** "There's nothing anyone can do about it."

10 When the man says, "I guess I'm going a little overboard," he means, ...

  a "I'm making this too important."   **b** "I'm not interested in this issue."

E GROUP WORK Answer each question and explain your answers. Listen again if you disagree.

Conversation 1

1 What does the man think we can do about crime?

2 Why does the woman think he is practical?

3 Which speaker's outlook is closer to yours, the man's or the woman's?

Conversation 2

1 What reasons do the speakers give for why so many people will get the Marburg virus sooner or later?

2 Which speaker is more optimistic—the man or the woman?

3 Which speaker's outlook is closer to yours, the man's or the woman's?

Conversation 3

1 What does the woman think we can do about terrorism?

2 Which speaker has a more realistic outlook—the man or the woman?

3 Which speaker's outlook is closer to yours, the man's or the woman's?

NOW YOU CAN Compare perspectives on world problems

A NOTEPADDING Write a list of world problems that you worry about. Or use the ideas in the pictures. Write why you worry about them.

Epidemics: I worry that we won't have enough medicines, and lots of people will die.

War

Drug trafficking

Political corruption

Public sanitation

Global warming

RECYCLE THIS LANGUAGE

· It's just a matter of time until …
· I mean, what are you going to do?
· These things are just part of life.
· You've got to roll with the punches.
· You're just a sitting duck.
· It is what it is.
· It's started getting to me.
· Better safe than sorry.

B DISCUSSION Meet with classmates who listed the same problems on their notepads. Discuss the problem and explain why you worry about it, providing details of experiences you or others you know have had with it. Discuss what, if anything, can be done about the problem.

A **READING WARM-UP** In what ways can a person's attitude help in solving a problem or achieving a goal?

B ▶1:11 **READING** Read the newspaper article, which is based on a true story in the news. What was Phil Cooper's mistake?

DAILY NEWS

August 7

FACEBOOK SAVES THE DAY

WESTON—In a painful ending to an otherwise glorious vacation, Phil and Virginia Cooper and their daughters, Miranda and Grace, arrived home without the hundreds of vacation snapshots they had taken.

"We'll always have our memories," said Phil, "but no pictures of our family's activities or the beautiful New England scenery and Cape Cod beaches where we spent the last two weeks of our summer vacation."

"Phil has always been a little absent-minded, but this takes the cake," Virginia said with an affectionate smile. "We were getting settled in the car for the long drive home, and Phil got out to snap one last picture of the sunset. Then he set the camera on the roof of the car while he got his jacket out of the trunk." Needless to say, the camera fell off the car as they drove off. The family discovered the camera was missing when they got home. Then Phil suddenly remembered placing the camera on the top of the car.

"I felt terrible for having been so careless and was sure the situation was

hopeless. Days had passed. The camera would have been lying on the ground through bad weather, or perhaps someone had found it and taken it home," Phil said. The camera case had the Coopers' name and address, but the camera hadn't been in the case.

Last weekend, while training for an Ironman Triathlon event, Adam Secrest, 24, spotted the camera along the side of Callman Road near Barton Beach, Massachusetts. He picked it up, looked for a name, and finding none, stashed it in his car, thinking he would try to locate the owner after his run. Once home, Secrest turned on the camera and scrolled through the photos.

"I felt sort of like a snoop, but my spying was purposeful," he said. "I was looking for clues to the owner's identity, and I was optimistic that I would find something."

Soon he came across a photo of two young girls getting on a yellow school bus with the words WESTON, NJ on the side. In a burst of creative thinking, Secrest thought someone might recognize the girls, so he posted the photo on Facebook and urged his friends to share it, with this message:
Do you know these kids from Weston, New Jersey? I found a camera with this photo in Barton, Massachusetts, and want to locate the owner. Please share.

Facebook friends shared the photo hundreds of times. It was just a matter of time until it appeared on the Weston Community page and someone recognized Miranda and Grace and called Virginia Cooper, who contacted Secrest, first through Facebook, and then by phone. The camera arrived at the Coopers' house by mail yesterday.

"Lots of people say social media is a meaningless waste of time, but here's an example of how powerful and useful it can be," said Secrest.

C **DETERMINE THE MAIN IDEA** Which statement expresses the main idea of the article?

1 There's nothing worse than losing one's vacation memories.

2 Creative thinking can help solve problems in unexpected ways.

3 Being a forgetful person can cause a lot of problems.

D **UNDERSTAND MEANING FROM CONTEXT** Locate these adjectives and expressions in the article and classify them as positive (+) or negative (-). Then, with a partner, try to explain the meaning of each one in your own words.

☐ absent-minded   ☐ hopeless   ☐ meaningless   ☐ useful
☐ affectionate   ☐ purposeful   ☐ powerful

E **SUMMARIZE** Read the article again. Then close your book and, with a partner, summarize the story in your own words.

F ▶ 1:12 **WORD STUDY   ADJECTIVE SUFFIXES -FUL AND -LESS**   Expand your vocabulary by learning these adjectives from the Reading on page 10 with the suffixes -ful (meaning "with") and -less (meaning "without"). Write one sentence using one of each pair.

-ful	-less	My sentence
careful	careless	....
hopeful	hopeless	....
meaningful	meaningless	....
painful	painless	....
powerful	powerless	....
purposeful	purposeless	....
useful	useless	....

G **WORD STUDY PRACTICE**   The following pairs of words aren't opposite equivalents. With a partner, discuss the difference in meaning of the words in these pairs.

> **Be careful!**
> Not all words that end in -ful and -less are opposite equivalents. Restful refers to a calm place or an experience, while restless refers to a person's feeling of physical nervousness. Always check the dictionary to confirm meaning.

restful / restless: We had a very restful vacation and didn't do much. / I was so restless last night. I couldn't sleep.

helpful / helpless: Your brother is so helpful. He always offers to do the chores at home. / Babies are so helpless. They can't do anything for themselves.

pitiful / pitiless: It was pitiful to see that poor cat looking for food. / How can people be so pitiless that they'd let a cat starve?

NOW YOU CAN   Discuss creative ways to achieve a goal

A **NOTEPADDING**   Adam Secrest's goal was to find the camera's owner. With a partner, brainstorm and write creative ways to achieve the goals on the notepad.

B **DISCUSSION**   Choose one goal and in a small group discuss ways to achieve it, based on your ideas from Exercise A. Present your ideas to the class.

> 66 Not everyone will want to donate a lot of money. So it's important to keep a positive attitude. If everyone gives a little, or donates time to help, we can still reach our goal. 99

OPTIONAL WRITING   In a paragraph, present the ideas you developed in Exercise B.

Goals:

To collect money for a good cause

To locate an organ donor for a sick person

To warn people about a danger

To find a lost person

To spread a political message

A WRITING SKILL   Study the rules.

A paragraph consists of sentences about one topic. The most important sentence in a paragraph is the **topic sentence**. It is often (though not always) the first sentence, and it introduces, states, or summarizes the topic of a paragraph. For example: Workaholics lead unbalanced lives.

In formal or academic writing, all the **supporting sentences** that follow, surround, or precede a topic sentence—details, examples, and other facts—must be related to the topic presented in the topic sentence.

If the last sentence of a paragraph isn't its topic sentence, and especially if the paragraph is a long one, writers sometimes end it with a **concluding sentence** that restates the topic sentence or summarizes the paragraph. Concluding sentences commonly use phrases such as <u>In conclusion</u> or <u>In summary</u>.

WRITING MODEL

Workaholics lead unbalanced lives. They spend all their energy on work. They rarely take time to relax and let their minds rest. I know, because my father was a workaholic, and he worked every day of the week. We hardly ever saw him. Even when he was not at work, we knew he was thinking about work. He seemed never to think of anything else. **In summary, not knowing how to escape from work makes it difficult for a workaholic to find balance in his or her life.**

B PRACTICE   The sentences below form a paragraph, but they are out of order. Write <u>T</u> next to the topic sentence, <u>S</u> next to each of the four supporting sentences, and <u>C</u> next to the concluding sentence. Then, on a separate sheet of paper, put the sentences in order and rewrite the paragraph.

.... **1** She took a night-shift job so she didn't have to do much work.

.... **2** Since they're very intelligent, some figure out how to do less work.

.... **3** Very intelligent people, or "brains," are sometimes lazy people.

.... **4** I had a friend who was a member of Mensa, an organization for people who are really smart.

.... **5** To sum up, sometimes intelligent people use their intelligence to get out of doing work.

.... **6** She could read novels most of the night and still get a paycheck.

C PRACTICE   Read the two paragraphs. Find and underline the topic sentence and the concluding sentence in each paragraph.

Terrorist acts take many forms, but all have one thing in common: the senseless targeting of innocent people to achieve maximum pain, fear, and disruption. In one type of act, a terrorist kills or harms a single individual for no apparent reason. In others, terrorists detonate explosives or bombs in crowded markets or at public events. In still others, terrorists attack public transportation, harming or killing many people at once. In conclusion, although I generally have a positive outlook, I think it is just a matter of time until terrorists harm me or people I know and love.

The things that worry many people don't worry me. For example, many people worry about war, epidemics, and natural catastrophes, such as storms and earthquakes. An individual person can't do anything about war, so why worry about it? I believe in hoping for the best. Epidemics can be terrible, but I trust in modern medicine and think scientists are doing everything they can to discover vaccines and treatments for them. And storms and earthquakes are relatively rare and can't be prevented, so it's best just to keep an optimistic outlook. Of course it would be silly not to take precautions that can help. "Better safe than sorry," as they say, but in most cases it's best just to try to roll with the punches.

D APPLY THE WRITING SKILL   Choose one (or more) world problems that worry you. Write a paragraph describing your outlook and attitude about the problem. Use the writing models in Exercise C as an example.

DIGITAL WRITING PROCESS

SELF-CHECK

☐ Does my paragraph have a topic sentence?

☐ Do the supporting sentences in my paragraph all relate to the topic?

☐ Do I have a concluding sentence?

A ▶ 1:13 Listen to the people talking about their reactions to events in the news. Decide if each speaker is an optimist, a pessimist, or a realist.

1 John ....   2 Susan ....   3 Matt ....

B Now read the statements. Write the name of the person from the listening who is most likely to have said each statement. Listen again if necessary.

1 "You've got to be practical. There will be some problems in life that you can solve and some that you can't. What's important is realizing when something is beyond your control. I mean, it is what it is." ....

2 "Life is full of hard times. Bad things happen and there's very little you can do about it." ....

3 "It's important to see a problem as both a challenge and an opportunity for success. Difficult experiences can make a person stronger." ....

C Complete each description in your own words.

1 An easygoing person is someone who ....

2 An outgoing person is someone who ....

3 A reliable person is someone who ....

4 A helpful person is someone who ....

D Complete each conversation with one of the words that describe behavior from page 6.

1 **A:** Looks like I have to work overtime again tonight. My boss just gave me three projects to complete by the end of the day.

   B: You're kidding. He sounds like a real .... !

2 **A:** You know, without Sarah's help, I would never have completed that presentation in time.

   B: Tell me about it. She really helped me out with my sales campaign last month. She's such a ....

3 **A:** Tom is really a .... I ran into him in the park last weekend, and he was sitting on a bench and working on that report.

   B: Yeah, that's Tom all right. He never stops!

4 **A:** I don't think Jill had a very good time at the party—she didn't say a word the whole evening.

   B: Well, Jill doesn't feel comfortable in social situations. She's just not a ....

E Complete each sentence with one of the adjectives from Word Study on page 11.

1 Excellent dental anesthesia today makes almost all dental treatment ....

2 Sometimes we feel completely .... ; there's just nothing we can do to make something happen.

3 The Internet can be very .... in helping us communicate with a large number of people at once.

4 I'm .... about the future. I think things will change for the better.

5 Some say the colors of a painting create a more .... impression than the black and white of a pencil drawing.

TEST-TAKING SKILLS BOOSTER   p. 151

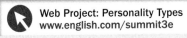
Web Project: Personality Types
www.english.com/summit3e

2 Music and Other Arts

COMMUNICATION GOALS

1 Describe how you've been enjoying the arts
2 Express a negative opinion politely
3 Describe a creative personality
4 Discuss the benefits of the arts

PREVIEW

A **FRAME YOUR IDEAS** Complete the survey. Then tell a partner about the songs and artists you listed. Explain why each one is memorable for you.

WRITE ONE OR MORE EXAMPLES OF YOUR

MUSICAL MEMORIES

1 A song with a really danceable beat that made you want to get up and move to the music

2 A song with a catchy, unforgettable melody that you loved—you couldn't get the music out of your head

3 A song with an annoying melody that drove you crazy every time you heard it

4 A song with really moving lyrics—you got emotional every time you heard the words

5 A song with interesting lyrics that made you really think about the song's meaning

6 A group or performer with an innovative sound unlike anything you'd heard before

7 A singer that blew you away with his or her extraordinary singing voice

8 A top-notch musician you thought was one of the most talented artists ever

9 A singer, musician, or group that put on an amazing and memorable performance

B ▶ 1:14 **VOCABULARY** **ELEMENTS OF MUSIC** Work with a partner to explain the meanings of the words on the right. Use the survey to support your explanation. Then listen and repeat.

a beat	a sound
a melody	a voice
lyrics	a performance

C **PAIR WORK** Tell your partner about the performers you'd like to see, or not like to see, in the future. Explain your reasons.

❝I'd love to see Bastille. They have a really unique sound.❞

D ▶ 1:15 **SPOTLIGHT** Read and listen to three colleagues discussing what to do after a meeting. Notice the spotlighted language.

ENGLISH FOR TODAY'S WORLD
Understand a variety of accents.
Amalia = Spanish
Sandy = Chinese
Paul = American English (standard)

Amalia: Hey, guys, we've got a free evening tonight. Why don't we see if there's anything to do?

Sandy: Good idea! Let me see if I can find something online.

Paul: **I'm in** … Check out eTix. They usually have some great deals.

Sandy: Let's see … Hey, *The Phantom of the Opera* is at the Palladium. I saw the movie, but I've never seen it live. What do you think?

Paul: I saw it back home in Chicago at least ten years ago. Hasn't that thing been playing for like twenty years now?

Amalia: At least! I've actually seen it on stage. But I guess I wouldn't mind seeing it again. The music is awesome.

Paul: Yeah, it's got some catchy melodies, but the story**'s nothing to write home about**.

Sandy: Hey, here's something that might be good! It looks like tickets are still available for *Swan Lake*. That's supposed to be an amazing ballet.

Paul: Uh, no offense, but ballet **isn't my thing**.

Amalia: I can see Paul's going to be **hard to please**!

Paul: Sorry, **I don't mean to be a pain**. I guess I'm not really in the mood for a show tonight. Maybe there's a museum that stays open late.

Sandy: Hold on! Here's something that might be **right up your alley**, Paul. There's an exhibit of modern American art at the Grant Gallery. And they're open late on Thursdays.

Paul: **Now you're talking!**

Sandy: And what I really love is the location. The gallery's right around the corner from here.

E **UNDERSTAND IDIOMS AND EXPRESSIONS** Find these expressions in Spotlight. Match each with its correct usage.

.... **1** I'm in.

.... **2** It's nothing to write home about.

.... **3** It isn't my thing.

.... **4** He's hard to please.

.... **5** I don't mean to be a pain.

.... **6** It's right up your alley.

.... **7** Now you're talking.

a You think someone will definitely be interested in something.

b You want to apologize for making trouble.

c You think someone has made a good suggestion.

d You think someone is difficult to satisfy.

e You think there's nothing special about something.

f You want to indicate your willingness to participate.

g You indicate that something isn't to your personal taste.

F **THINK AND EXPLAIN** Discuss these questions.

1 Who's willing to see *The Phantom of the Opera* and who's not? Explain each person's point of view.

2 Why do you think Sandy thinks the art exhibit might be just right for Paul?

SPEAKING **PAIR WORK** Rate the events on a scale of 1 to 5 (with 5 being most enjoyable). Then tell your partner about the kinds of events you'd like to attend. Explain your reasons in detail.

> ❝ Musicals aren't really my thing. They just seem silly to me. But a rock concert's right up my alley. ❞

☐ an art exhibit   ☐ a modern dance performance   ☐ a play

☐ a rock concert   ☐ a classical music concert   ☐ a musical

☐ a comedy show   ☐ a jazz performance   ☐ a ballet

GOAL Describe how you've been enjoying the arts

A ▶ 1:16 **GRAMMAR SPOTLIGHT** Read the commentaries. Notice the spotlighted grammar.

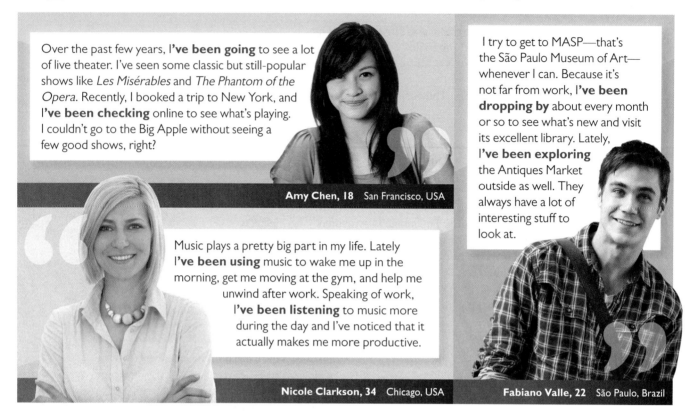

Over the past few years, **I've been going** to see a lot of live theater. I've seen some classic but still-popular shows like *Les Misérables* and *The Phantom of the Opera*. Recently, I booked a trip to New York, and **I've been checking** online to see what's playing. I couldn't go to the Big Apple without seeing a few good shows, right?

Amy Chen, 18 San Francisco, USA

I try to get to MASP—that's the São Paulo Museum of Art—whenever I can. Because it's not far from work, **I've been dropping by** about every month or so to see what's new and visit its excellent library. Lately, **I've been exploring** the Antiques Market outside as well. They always have a lot of interesting stuff to look at.

Music plays a pretty big part in my life. Lately **I've been using** music to wake me up in the morning, get me moving at the gym, and help me unwind after work. Speaking of work, **I've been listening** to music more during the day and I've noticed that it actually makes me more productive.

Nicole Clarkson, 34 Chicago, USA

Fabiano Valle, 22 São Paulo, Brazil

B **MAKE PERSONAL COMPARISONS** Which person's tastes, interests, and activities are the most like (or the least like) your own? Explain why.

DIGITAL
INDUCTIVE
ACTIVITY

C **GRAMMAR** THE PRESENT PERFECT CONTINUOUS

Use the present perfect continuous to express a continuing action that began in the past and continues in the present. Depending on the context, the action may continue in the future. Use <u>have</u> / <u>has</u> + <u>been</u> and a present participle.

Statements
She**'s been practicing** ballet for years.
I**'ve been listening** to classical music since I was a kid.

Questions
Have you **been playing** the piano for a long time?
How long **has** your son **been painting** portraits?

These words and phrases are often used with the present perfect continuous (and the present perfect) when describing continuing actions:

for [two months]	lately	these days
for a while	recently	this [year]
since [2013]	all day	How long ... ?

Note: The present perfect continuous, rather than the present perfect, is generally used to describe a recent continuous action, especially when there is visible evidence that the action has just ended.

What's Nora's violin doing on the table? **Has** she **been practicing**?

Remember:
The present perfect can also be used to describe a continuing action that began in the past. There is no significant difference in meaning.

She**'s practiced** ballet for years.
I**'ve listened** to classical music since I was a kid.
Have you **played** the piano for a long time?
How long **has** your son **painted** portraits?

However, use the present perfect, not the present perfect continuous, in sentences with <u>already</u>, <u>yet</u>, <u>before</u>, and <u>ever</u>, because they describe finished actions.

She**'s already practiced** ballet this week.
Have you **ever studied** piano?

GRAMMAR BOOSTER p. 126
Finished and unfinished actions: summary

D **NOTICE THE GRAMMAR** Find an example of the present perfect continuous in Spotlight on page 15. Does it describe an action that has finished or one that may continue in the future?

E **UNDERSTAND THE GRAMMAR** Check the sentences in which the present perfect continuous can also be used. Then, on a separate sheet of paper, rewrite those sentences in the present perfect continuous.

☐ **1** He's played with their band for almost ten years.

☐ **2** Justin Timberlake has already given two concerts in my town.

☐ **3** She's looked online this morning for a good deal on show tickets.

☐ **4** Since he got promoted to stage manager, Mark's arrived early at the theater every day.

☐ **5** We've gone to a lot of concerts lately.

☐ **6** Have you ever visited the Museum of Contemporary Art?

☐ **7** How many times have you seen the musical *Les Misérables*?

☐ **8** Lately, audiences have asked them to play more songs from their new album.

F **GRAMMAR PRACTICE** Complete the questions, using the present perfect continuous when possible. Otherwise, use the present perfect.

1 A: .... music videos on my tablet?
   you / watch

   B: Yes, I have. But I'm done.

2 A: .... the musical *Wicked* yet?
   Max / see

   B: No, he hasn't. But he should. It's unforgettable.

3 A: .... ?
   what / you / do

   B: Just now? I've been checking to see if there are any interesting art exhibits this week.

4 A: .... late again?
   Vickie / work

   B: I'm afraid so. But she'll be heading home in a few minutes.

5 A: .... to a Broadway musical?
   Jerry / go

   B: Never. But he's going to his first one tonight.

6 A: .... in line to get in to the concert?
   how long / you / wait

   B: About twenty minutes. But it looks like we're finally moving now.

PRONUNCIATION BOOSTER	p. 142
Intonation patterns	

NOW YOU CAN Describe how you've been enjoying the arts

A **NOTEPADDING** Write about your experiences with the arts recently. Explain why you've been doing some things and not doing others. Use the present perfect continuous.

Music	Art
I've been listening to a lot of jazz these days. It helps me unwind.	I haven't been going to any art exhibits lately. But to tell the truth, it's not really my thing.

Music	Art	Theater

B **DISCUSSION ACTIVATOR** Discuss the role the arts have been playing in your life recently. Use your notes to discuss what you've been doing (or not doing) lately. Ask your partner questions. Say as much as you can.

❝ Have you been going to many plays or musicals recently? ❞

GOAL Express a negative opinion politely

 A ► 1:17 **VOCABULARY** NEGATIVE DESCRIPTIONS OF MUSIC

Read and listen. Then listen again and repeat.

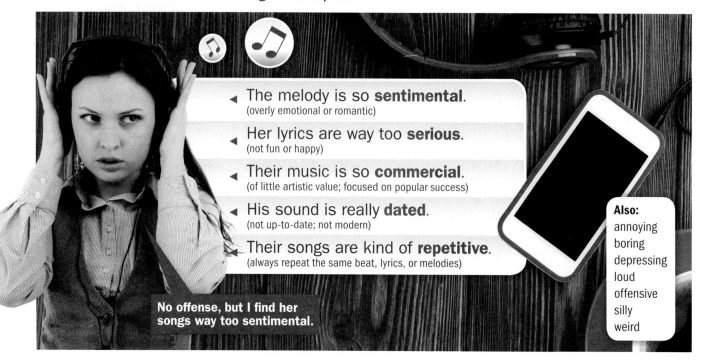

◄ The melody is so **sentimental**.
(overly emotional or romantic)

◄ Her lyrics are way too **serious**.
(not fun or happy)

◄ Their music is so **commercial**.
(of little artistic value; focused on popular success)

◄ His sound is really **dated**.
(not up-to-date; not modern)

◄ Their songs are kind of **repetitive**.
(always repeat the same beat, lyrics, or melodies)

Also:
annoying
boring
depressing
loud
offensive
silly
weird

No offense, but I find her
songs way too sentimental.

B ► 1:18 **LISTEN TO ACTIVATE VOCABULARY** Listen to each conversation. Then complete the description.

1 He finds Jackie Evancho's music way too (repetitive / commercial / sentimental / serious).

2 She finds Maná very (repetitive / commercial / dated / serious).

3 He finds Caetano Veloso a little too (repetitive / sentimental / dated / serious).

4 She thinks reggae music is really (repetitive / sentimental / dated / commercial).

5 He thinks Anthony Hopkins's music is too (repetitive / sentimental / dated / serious).

C **APPLY THE VOCABULARY** With a partner, describe singers and bands you don't like, using the Vocabulary.

❝In my opinion, Phil Collins's music is way too commercial. And I hate to say it, but it's pretty dated, too. Do you agree?❞

 D **GRAMMAR** CLEFT SENTENCES WITH <u>WHAT</u>

One way to emphasize the action in a sentence is to use a noun clause with <u>What</u> as the subject of the sentence + the verb <u>be</u>. Make sure the form of the verb <u>be</u> agrees with its complement.

Cleft sentences

(**I really don't like** traditional music.) → **What I really don't like is** traditional music.

(**He doesn't understand** jazz.) → **What he doesn't understand is** jazz.

(**They really loved** the lyrics.) → **What they really loved were** the lyrics.

(The melody **made everyone cry**.) → **What made everyone cry was** the melody.

GRAMMAR BOOSTER p. 128
· Noun clauses: review and expansion
· Noun clauses as adjective and noun complements

 E **NOTICE THE GRAMMAR** Find an example of a cleft sentence with <u>What</u> in Spotlight on page 15.

F GRAMMAR PRACTICE Rewrite each statement as a cleft sentence with <u>What</u>.

1 I can't stand long classical music concerts. ....*What I can't stand are long classical music concerts.*....

2 I didn't care for Adele's overly sentimental lyrics. ....

3 Jessica doesn't particularly like Bono's voice. ....

4 I'd really enjoy seeing a live Lady Gaga performance. ....

5 The song "I Gotta Feeling" by the Black Eyed Peas really makes me want to dance. ....
....

G PAIR WORK Take turns reading a statement aloud. Your partner restates it as a cleft sentence with <u>What</u>.

1 "Jazz always puts me to sleep."
2 "I can't stand the loud beat in techno-pop."
3 "A good melody can make even bad lyrics seem acceptable."
4 "Listening to my brother try to sing drives me crazy."
5 "Dancing to the music of a great salsa band helps me unwind."
6 "I love downloading songs by unknown new artists."

NOW YOU CAN Express a negative opinion politely

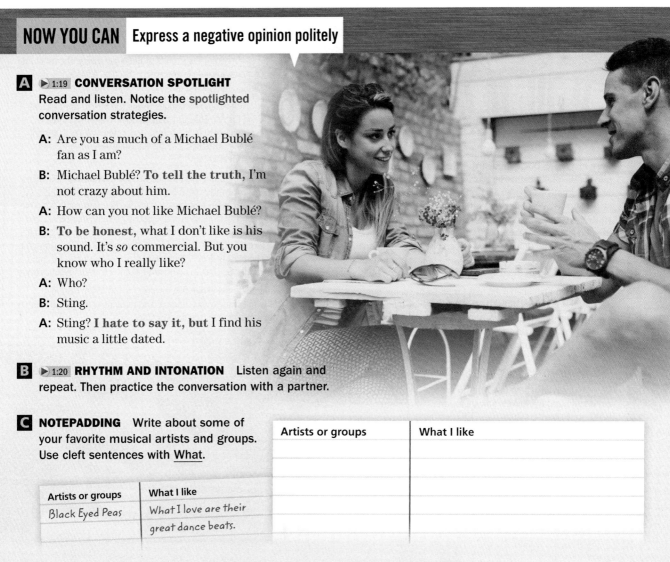

A ▶ 1:19 **CONVERSATION SPOTLIGHT**
Read and listen. Notice the spotlighted
conversation strategies.

A: Are you as much of a Michael Bublé
fan as I am?

B: Michael Bublé? **To tell the truth,** I'm
not crazy about him.

A: How can you not like Michael Bublé?

B: **To be honest,** what I don't like is his
sound. It's *so* commercial. But you
know who I really like?

A: Who?

B: Sting.

A: Sting? **I hate to say it, but** I find his
music a little dated.

B ▶ 1:20 **RHYTHM AND INTONATION** Listen again and
repeat. Then practice the conversation with a partner.

C NOTEPADDING Write about some of
your favorite musical artists and groups.
Use cleft sentences with <u>What</u>.

Artists or groups	What I like

Artists or groups	What I like
Black Eyed Peas	What I love are their great dance beats.

D CONVERSATION ACTIVATOR Create a conversation similar
to the one in Exercise A. Start like this: *Are you as much of a
__ fan as I am?* Be sure to change roles and then partners.

DON'T STOP!
• Discuss other artists
you like or don't like.
• Say as much as you can.

19

A ▶ 1:21 **VOCABULARY**   **DESCRIBING CREATIVE PERSONALITIES**
Read and listen. Then listen again and repeat.

Positive qualities		Negative qualities	
gifted	having a natural ability to do one or more things extremely well	**eccentric**	behaving in an unusual way or appearing different from most people
energetic	very active, physically and mentally	**difficult**	never satisfied and hard to please
imaginative	able to think of new and interesting ideas	**moody**	becoming quickly and easily annoyed or unhappy
passionate	showing a strong liking for something and being very dedicated to it	**egotistical**	believing oneself to be better or more important than other people

B **READING WARM-UP**   It is often said that gifted people have eccentric, moody, or difficult personalities. Do you agree? Explain.

C ▶ 1:22 **READING**   Read the short biography. What effect did Beethoven's personality have on his life?

A Passionate Genius

Born in 1770 in Bonn, Germany, Ludwig van Beethoven started playing the piano before he was four years old. Clearly gifted, he had already composed his first piece of music by the time he was twelve. When Beethoven was just sixteen, he went to study in Vienna, Austria, then the center of European cultural life and home to the most brilliant musicians and composers of the period. Beethoven proved to be both a gifted pianist and an imaginative composer. He went on to create his own unique sound and melodies loved by millions.

Beethoven is remembered not only for his great genius, but also for his strong and difficult personality. In one infamous incident, Beethoven became so annoyed with a waiter that he emptied a plate of food over the man's head. He could also be quite egotistical, saying once, "There are and will be thousands of princes. There is only one Beethoven." During concerts, if people talked while he was performing, he would stop and walk out.

Despite this type of behavior, many in musical and aristocratic circles admired Beethoven, and music lovers were always Beethoven's greatest supporters. This fact did not prevent him from losing his temper with one or another of them. However, because of his talent, Beethoven's friends always forgave his insults and moody temperament.

In addition to being difficult, Beethoven was also well-known for his eccentric behavior. He had the odd habit of putting his head in cold water before he composed any music. He often walked through the streets of Vienna muttering to himself and stamping his feet. He completely neglected his personal appearance; he had wild hair, and his clothes would get so dirty that his friends would come during the night and replace his old clothes with new ones. What amazed his friends was that he never noticed the difference.

Beethoven wrote two famous works, *Moonlight Sonata* and *Für Elise*, for two different women he loved. He was almost always passionately in love, often with a woman who was already married or engaged. Although Beethoven asked several women to marry him, they all rejected him.

The most tragic aspect of Beethoven's life was his gradual loss of hearing, beginning in his late twenties until he became completely deaf in his forties. However, even as his hearing grew worse, Beethoven continued to be energetic and productive; his creative activity remained intense, and audiences were deeply touched by his music. In 1826, Beethoven held his last public performance of his famous *Ninth Symphony*. By this time, the composer was completely deaf. When he was turned around so he could see the roaring applause that he could not hear, Beethoven began to cry.

Beethoven died in Vienna at age fifty-seven. One out of ten people who lived in Vienna came to his funeral. And millions of people all over the world have been enjoying his music ever since.

D **INFER INFORMATION**   Infer the information from the Reading. Explain your answers.

1 the year Beethoven moved away from Bonn

2 Beethoven's age when he gave his last public performance

3 the reason he cried

4 the year Beethoven died

E **IDENTIFY SUPPORTING DETAILS**   On a separate sheet of paper, write examples from the Reading of Beethoven's behavior that illustrate each personality trait. Use your own words. Explain your answers.

1 that he was gifted
2 that he was energetic
3 that he was imaginative

4 that he was passionate
5 that he was eccentric
6 that he was difficult

7 that he was moody
8 that he was egotistical

F **EXPRESS AND SUPPORT AN OPINION**   Discuss the questions. Activate the Vocabulary to support your opinion.

1 Why do you think every woman that Beethoven asked to marry him rejected him? Do you think they made the right decision?

DIGITAL
EXTRA
CHALLENGE

2 Why do you think Beethoven was able to write some of his most popular pieces of music when he could no longer hear?

NOW YOU CAN   Describe a creative personality

A **FRAME YOUR IDEAS**   Do you think you have a creative personality? Rate yourself for the qualities below on a scale from 0 to 3. Compare answers with a partner.

> **""** I'm not particularly creative, but I'm very **passionate**. I think it's really important to love what you do. What about you? **""**

0 = not at all	
1 = a little	
2 = somewhat	
3 = extremely	

...... gifted   ...... difficult
...... eccentric   ...... energetic
...... passionate   ...... moody
...... imaginative   ...... egotistical

B **DISCUSSION**   Provide details to complete the descriptions of these creative personalities, or write complete descriptions of others you find interesting. Be sure to use the Vocabulary and provide examples. Say as much as you can.

Michael Jackson was a gifted singer, songwriter, and dancer from the U.S. But a lot of people found him eccentric. For example, ...

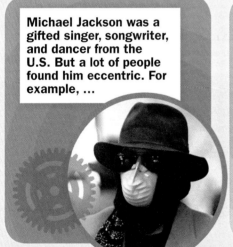

Frida Kahlo was a famous Mexican painter. They say that, at times, she could be quite moody. For example, ...

Christian Bale is a Hollywood actor who is originally from the U.K. He is very talented and is known to be very passionate about acting. But it is said that he can be egotistical and difficult to work with. For example, ...

OPTIONAL WRITING   Write a biography of a creative person. Present it to the class.

RECYCLE THIS LANGUAGE	
• a pain in the neck	• a team player
• a people person	• a tyrant
• a sweetheart	• a workaholic

A **LISTENING WARM-UP** **DISCUSSION** In what ways do you think the arts could be used to help children who are under emotional stress or the elderly with memory problems?

DIGITAL STRATEGIES **B** ▶ 1:23 **LISTEN FOR MAIN IDEAS** Listen to the radio program for descriptions of how the arts are used as therapy. Write the type of therapy that is described by each therapist.

Mark Branch 1 .... Bruce Nelson 2 .... Carla Burgess 3 ....

C ▶ 1:24 **LISTEN FOR SUPPORTING INFORMATION** Listen to the radio program again and complete each statement. Then explain what the therapist does to achieve each goal.

1 Mark Branch uses the arts to help patients with intellectual disabilities improve ....
  a their schoolwork   **b** their ability to socialize

2 Bruce Nelson uses the arts to help troubled teens ....
  a talk about their problems more easily   **b** socialize with others more easily

3 Carla Burgess uses the arts to help the elderly ....
  a tell others about their problems   **b** socialize with others

D ▶ 1:25 **LISTEN TO TAKE NOTES** Listen to the radio program again. Work with a partner to define these words and phrases.

1 an intellectual disability: ....

2 a troubled teen: ....

3 a senior: ....

E **APPLY IDEAS** Read each situation. Which therapies mentioned in the radio program would *you* recommend for each situation and why? Compare and discuss your answers with a partner.

1 A number of humanitarian organizations have been working with children who were forced to become soldiers and fight in local wars. In many cases these children have participated in violent acts. Their experiences make it hard to sleep or interact normally with others.

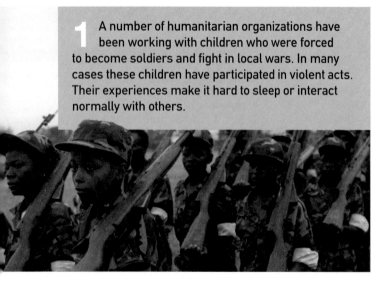

2 Greenwood Hospital specializes in helping patients who have been in car accidents and sports- or work-related accidents. Patients struggle with physical pain, limited movement in arms and legs, and depression. They need emotional support.

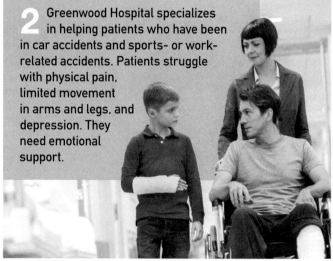

3 The Walker Institute provides support for adults who have suddenly found themselves without a job or a place to live. As a result, these people feel separated from others socially. Understandably, they feel bad about their current circumstances and worry a lot about the future.

DIGITAL STRATEGIES **F WORD STUDY** USING PARTICIPIAL ADJECTIVES

> The present and past participial forms of many verbs can function as adjectives.
>
> The past participle has a passive meaning. It can usually be restated with a <u>by</u> phrase.
>
> > The patient is **depressed** [by his life].
> > I'm **bored** [by this movie].
>
> The present participle does not have a passive meaning. It can usually be restated with an active verb.
>
> > That book is **depressing**. [It depresses everyone.]
> > It's so **boring**. [It bores me.]

▶ 1:26 Participial adjectives

Verb	Present participle	Past participle
(amaze)	amazing	amazed
(annoy)	annoying	annoyed
(bore)	boring	bored
(depress)	depressing	depressed
(disappoint)	disappointing	disappointed
(entertain)	entertaining	entertained
(excite)	exciting	excited
(interest)	interesting	interested
(please)	pleasing	pleased
(relax)	relaxing	relaxed
(soothe)	soothing	soothed
(stimulate)	stimulating	stimulated
(surprise)	surprising	surprised
(touch)	touching	touched
(trouble)	troubling	troubled

G WORD STUDY PRACTICE Circle an adjective to complete each sentence.

1 Music can make language students feel (relaxed / relaxing).

2 Drawing pictures about their problems can make patients feel less (depressed / depressing).

3 Some patients find movement therapy to be very (soothed / soothing).

4 For patients in physical pain, the benefits of music therapy can be (surprised / surprising).

5 Researchers are (amazed / amazing) that the results have been so positive.

6 Many doctors report they are (pleased / pleasing) with the progress their patients make.

7 Many teen patients feel that drama therapy is (entertained / entertaining).

H WORD STUDY PRACTICE With a partner, take turns choosing a present participial adjective from Exercise F and using it in a sentence. Your partner then creates a sentence using the past participial form.

> ❝I think music therapy might be **disappointing**. ❞

> ❝I think I might be **disappointed** by music therapy. ❞

NOW YOU CAN Discuss the benefits of the arts

A NOTEPADDING What are some benefits that music, art, dance, and theater bring to people's everyday lives? With a partner, make a list and discuss. Use participial adjectives.

Benefits	Examples
Music can be soothing.	Playing music at work relaxes people so they're more productive.

Benefits	Examples

DIGITAL SPEAKING BOOSTER **B GROUP WORK** Present your ideas to your class or group. Comment on your classmates' ideas and ask questions.

A WRITING SKILL Study the rules.

When listing two or more words in a series, be sure to use parallel structure. All the words, phrases, or clauses should be in the same form. Study the examples.

I like **dancing, painting**, and **singing**. (All are gerunds.)
I like **to dance, to paint**, and **to sing**. (All are infinitives.)
The picture **was painted, framed**, and **sold**. (All are passives.)
She's a **friendly, helpful**, and **intelligent** human being. (All are adjectives.)

If you are listing two or more infinitives, either use <u>to</u> with all of them or use it only with the first one.

She wants **to eat, to drink**, and **to go** to sleep. *OR* She wants **to eat, drink**, and **go** to sleep.

With a pair or series of nouns, either use the article with all of them, or use it only with the first one.

I'm **a student, a musician**, and **a mother**. *OR* I'm **a student, musician**, and **mother**.

If another word refers to all of the words in the series, you can use it with all of them or only with the first.

I don't think I'm **very interesting** or **very smart**. *OR* I don't think I'm **very interesting** or **smart**.
I prefer people **who make me laugh** and **who like outdoor activities**.
OR I prefer people **who make me laugh** and **like outdoor activities**.

B ERROR CORRECTION Find and correct the errors.

My personality

Some people think I am moody, a pessimistic person, and cautious, because I sometimes worry about the future. However, this is very surprising to me. What I think is that I have always been a passionate, a positive, and optimistic person. The fact that I love traveling, to meet new people, and learning about new places proves that I don't have a pessimistic outlook. Most of my friends find me to be energetic and imaginative.

C PRACTICE On a separate sheet of paper, complete each statement with the words in parentheses, using parallel structure. Then write at least two similar sentences about your own personality and interests.

1 I like (read, listen to music, go to movies).

2 I've been (teacher, stay-at-home mom, office manager).

3 I enjoy (hike, ski, swim in the ocean).

4 (see new places, have new experiences, make new friends) are all reasons I like to travel.

5 Last year I (join the volleyball team, play in ten games, win an award).

6 What energizes and relaxes me is (paint portraits, cook great meals, play my guitar).

D APPLY THE WRITING SKILL Write a paragraph describing your interests and personality. Try to include at least one sentence using the present perfect continuous and one using a cleft sentence with <u>What</u>. Use the Vocabulary from Units 1 and 2.

SELF-CHECK

☐ Does my paragraph have a topic sentence and supporting sentences?

☐ Do I have a concluding sentence?

☐ Did I use parallel structure?

A ▶ 1:27 Listen to the conversations about musical preferences. Check the person who doesn't like the music. Then listen again and write what the person doesn't like about it.

		The man	The woman	What he or she doesn't like
1	One Direction	☐	☐	....
2	Vanessa-Mae	☐	☐	....
3	Josh Groban	☐	☐	....
4	Lady Gaga	☐	☐	....
5	Antonio Carlos Jobim	☐	☐	....

B Complete the statements with an appropriate adjective from the box.

| eccentric | egotistical | energetic | gifted | moody | passionate |

1 Sarah is a very .... musician. She started playing the piano when she was three.

2 My neighbor has thirty cats. You could say he's a bit ....

3 Franco is an extremely .... person. He only thinks of himself.

4 Dalia has been so .... lately. She gets angry at the smallest thing.

5 My brother is really .... He's always doing something productive.

6 My boss is so .... about the products we sell. She really believes in them.

C Check the sentences in which the present perfect continuous or present perfect are used correctly. Correct and rewrite the incorrect sentences on a separate sheet of paper.

☐ 1 I've already been writing two reports for my boss this month.

☐ 2 Kate hasn't seen the movie *Interstellar* yet, but all her friends have been telling her how great it is.

☐ 3 They've never been hearing about art therapy before.

☐ 4 Most likely, Lance studied late. His bedroom light is still on.

☐ 5 We haven't been making reservations for our flight yet.

☐ 6 I'll bet you've done the laundry. I can hear the washing machine.

D Rewrite each statement as a cleft sentence with <u>What</u>.

1 Life without the arts wouldn't be much fun.

....

2 I don't like a band whose music is really commercial.

....

3 The beat made everyone feel like dancing.

....

4 I like to listen to music that has fun lyrics and a great melody.

....

5 They should go see anything that's playing on Broadway.

....

TEST-TAKING SKILLS BOOSTER p. 152

Web Project: Benefits of the Arts
www.english.com/summit3e

Money, Finance, and You

PREVIEW

A **FRAME YOUR IDEAS**   Take the test to learn about your personal spending style. Circle the letter that best describes you.

SPENDING HABITS SELF-TEST

1 **You hear about the latest (expensive!) smart phone with the coolest new features. You …**

A run to the store and stand in line to be one of the first people to have it.
B compare prices online so you can get the best deal right away.
C tell yourself that the price always comes down after a while and decide to wait.
D other _____

2 **You are invited to a birthday party and know a gift is expected, but you're short on cash right now. You …**

A spend more on the gift than you can afford anyway.
B try to find a nice gift that's not too expensive.
C say you are busy and don't go, so you don't have to buy a gift.
D other _____

3 **You discover a hole in your pants. You …**

A go out and buy new pants.
B have the pants repaired.
C fix the pants yourself.
D other _____

4 **You would love to have a fancy high-tech entertainment system in your living room, but you just don't have the money right now. You …**

A buy it with your credit card and hope you find the money to pay for it later.
B cut back on other expenses until you've saved enough to buy it.
C decide you have more important spending priorities than buying an entertainment system.
D other _____

5 **You always split the restaurant bill equally with two work colleagues when you eat lunch. This time you weren't hungry and ate very little. You …**

A pay your usual 1/3 of the bill.
B offer to pay for just the small amount you ate.
C ask the others to treat you, since your amount was so small.
D other _____

If you circled three or more A's:
You are definitely a big spender.
Your motto is:
Easy come, easy go.

If you circled three or more B's:
You've got a good head on your shoulders about money.
Your motto is:
Everything in moderation.

If you circled three or more C's:
You are thrifty and don't waste money.
Your motto is:
Waste not, want not.

If you wrote your own answers (D) for three or more questions:
How would you describe your spending style?

B ▶ 2:01 **VOCABULARY**   **DESCRIBING SPENDING STYLES**
Listen and repeat.

a big spender	a person who regularly spends a lot of money
thrifty	careful not to spend too much money
a cheapskate	a person who hates to spend money

C **DISCUSSION**   Do you know anyone you would call a big spender, thrifty, or a cheapskate? Give one or more examples of that person's behavior to support your opinion.

ENGLISH FOR TODAY'S WORLD
Understand a variety of accents.
Brad = American English (standard)
Brad's dad = American English (standard)

D ▶2:02 **SPOTLIGHT** Read and listen to a conversation between a father and son about spending. Notice the spotlighted language.

Brad: Dad! Check out the smart bikes! Are they cool, or what? And there's a place for your smart phone on the handlebars so you can get texts. You don't have to look for your phone while you're riding!

Dad: You've got to be kidding. "*Smart* bike"? Sounds more like a dumb bike. Don't tell me you text while you're riding your bike!

Brad: Oops. I shouldn't have said that. What I meant is that I could just stop and take a look.

Dad: Look. Even if this were a great bike, which it isn't, it's **way over our budget**. Look at the price—it's **astronomical**! And what's so special about it except for the ridiculous handlebars?—which should be illegal in my opinion …

Brad: Well, I could **chip in** part of the cost. I've **saved up a little for a rainy day**, like you've always told me to.

Dad: Hey, I'm really proud of you for not spending all your money. But this isn't a rainy day. The bike is a totally unnecessary

impulse item. They want you to buy it without thinking. And the handlebars are just a **gimmick** to get you to want it.

Brad: But for once, I'd like to be the *first* person to have something cool, you know?

Dad: Well, if you **have your heart set on** this smart bike, then you'll have to save up and pay for it yourself. But I'll need your **word of honor** you won't text while you're riding.

Brad: OK. But Dad, by the time I have enough money to buy a smart bike myself, all my friends will have already gotten theirs!

Dad: That may be true, but Mom and I won't **shell out** that much money for this bike, even if you do chip in. It's a **matter of principle**. You know, money doesn't grow on trees.

E **UNDERSTAND IDIOMS AND EXPRESSIONS** Match the expressions from Spotlight with their meaning.

.... **1** way over our budget
.... **2** astronomical
.... **3** chip in
.... **4** saved up a little for a rainy day
.... **5** impulse item
.... **6** gimmick
.... **7** have your heart set on
.... **8** word of honor
.... **9** shell out
.... **10** matter of principle

a promise
b very, very high
c more than we can spend
d pay
e contribute some of the cost
f kept some money in case of an emergency
g something you buy without thinking much about it
h something that's right
i a valueless feature
j really want

F **THINK AND EXPLAIN** Support your answers to the questions with information from Spotlight.

1 In your opinion, will Brad buy the smart bike for himself?

2 Do you think Brad sees his dad as a big spender, thrifty, or a cheapskate? How does his dad see him?.

SPEAKING **GROUP WORK** Discuss some worthless gimmicks and worthwhile features you've seen promoted for the following products.

1 an electronic product ....

2 a personal-care product ....

3 a shoe for a specific sport ....

4 another product ....

GOAL Express buyer's remorse

A ▶2:03 **VOCABULARY** EXPRESSING BUYER'S REMORSE

Read and listen. Then listen again and repeat.

It costs so much to maintain.

It takes up so much room.

It's so hard to operate.

It's so hard to put together.

It just sits around collecting dust.

B ▶2:04 **LISTEN FOR DETAILS** Listen to conversations about items people bought. Write the product they're discussing.

1 ....   3 ....   5 ....

2 ....   4 ....

C ▶2:05 **ACTIVATE VOCABULARY** Listen again. Pay attention to the people's regrets. From what they say, infer the reason for the regrets, using expressions from the Vocabulary. Use each Vocabulary expression only one time.

1 ...*It takes up too much room.*...............   4 ....

2 ....   5 ....

3 ....

D **GRAMMAR** EXPRESSING REGRETS ABOUT THE PAST

Wish + the past perfect

I **wish** I **had bought** a smart bike. And I **wish** I **hadn't bought** this car!
Do they **wish** they **had joined** a gym instead of buying that treadmill?
Don't you **wish** the store **had had** the uPhone a month ago?
Why does Ann **wish** she **had gotten** the more expensive model?

> **GRAMMAR BOOSTER** p. 129
> The past unreal conditional: inverted form

Should have or **ought to have** + past participle

I **should have waited** to buy a food processor = I **ought to have waited** to buy a food processor.

Note: American English speakers use <u>should have</u>, not <u>ought to have</u>, in negative statements and in questions.

He shouldn't have bought the shoes in size 40. NOT He ~~ought not to have bought~~ the shoes in size 40.
Should you have sold your house? NOT ~~Ought you to have sold~~ your house?

If only + the past perfect

Express very strong regret with <u>If only</u> + the past perfect. You can also use <u>if only</u> in a past unreal conditional statement and include a result clause.

If only I had bought an underwater camera! (regret: I wish I had.)
If only we hadn't bought that car! (regret: We wish we hadn't.)
If only I had bought an underwater camera, I **would have taken** pictures of the coral reef.

E **NOTICE THE GRAMMAR** Find one regret about the past in Spotlight on page 27.

F UNDERSTAND THE GRAMMAR   On a separate sheet of paper, rewrite the statements and questions, changing <u>wish</u> or <u>if only</u> + the past perfect to <u>should have</u> or <u>ought to have</u>.

1 She wishes she had bought a new car. (ought to)

> *She ought to have bought a new car.*

2 Do you wish you had read the owner's manual before you tried to use the espresso maker? (should)

3 We wish we had gone to a discount store instead of this fancy department store. (ought to)

4 If only I hadn't been in such a hurry to sell my house! (should)

5 Doesn't he wish he had taken the tutorial for his new computer? (should)

6 I wish I hadn't bought these gimmicky basketball shoes! (should)

G PAIR WORK   Read each quotation. Then take turns asking each question. Your partner answers with a statement using <u>wish</u> + the past perfect.

1 Steven said, "I should have exchanged those shoes." **What does Steven wish?**

> 66 He wishes he had exchanged those shoes. 99

2 Kate said, "I shouldn't have tried to repair this air-conditioner myself." **What does Kate wish?**

3 Michelle's husband said, "You should have bought a convertible." **What does Michelle's husband wish?**

4 Clark said, "My dad should have returned the defective tires as soon as he read about the problem in the news." **What does Clark wish?**

5 The teacher told Suzanne, "The kids ought to have taken the school bus this morning." **What does Suzanne's children's teacher wish?**

NOW YOU CAN   Express buyer's remorse

A ▶ 2:06 **CONVERSATION SPOTLIGHT**   Read and listen. Notice the spotlighted conversation strategies.

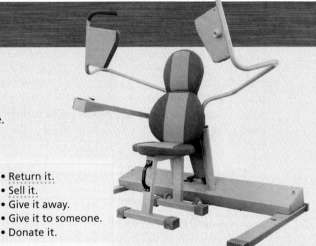

A: **You know,** I wish I hadn't gotten that exercise machine.

B: **What do you mean?**

A: Well, **I hate to say it, but** it's pretty hard to operate.

B: **That's a shame.** Can you return it?

A: It's too late. If only I'd thought about that sooner.

B: Well, maybe you can sell it.

A: **I'll think about that.** Thanks.

- Return it.
- Sell it.
- Give it away.
- Give it to someone.
- Donate it.

B ▶ 2:07 **RHYTHM AND INTONATION**   Listen again and repeat. Then practice the conversation with a partner.

C **NOTEPADDING**   Answer the questions on the notepad about something you regret buying.

What did you buy?

Do you still have it?

If not, what did you do with it?

Would you ever buy a similar item again?

DIGITAL VIDEO
DIGITAL SPEAKING BOOSTER

D **CONVERSATION ACTIVATOR**   Create a conversation expressing regret. Use the Vocabulary and the Grammar. Start like this: *You know, I wish…* Be sure to change roles and partners.

DON'T STOP!

- Make other suggestions about what to do with the item.
- Accept or decline the suggestion.
- If you decline, explain why.
- Say as much as you can.

GOAL Talk about financial goals and plans

A ▶ 2:08 **GRAMMAR SPOTLIGHT** Read the interview responses. Notice the spotlighted grammar.

Q: Tell us about your short-term and long-term financial goals and plans.

I've decided to set a long-term goal for myself—to save enough money to buy a new car. By this time next year, **I'll have put away** enough cash for a down payment. I'm optimistic that I'll be able to afford the monthly payments after that. My short-term goal is to make a budget for my monthly expenses and stick to it.

Hana Sung, 28
Incheon, South Korea

I find it helpful to try to picture where I want to be in the next few years. By next year, if I play my cards right, I figure **I'll have gotten** a good job as a financial consultant. That's a short-term plan, I guess. My long-term goals? They're still a little up in the air, but my goal is to be financially independent, able to retire if I want to, before I'm fifty.

Paul Drake, 24
Sydney, Australia

I'm not a big spender, but my college expenses have been astronomical, and now I'm in debt. My salary from my part-time job helps a bit, but I still had to borrow money from my family, and paying back those loans will take some time. Here's my plan: By this time next year, **I'll have graduated**. My immediate goal is to find a job and make enough money to be able to put away 10% every month, which I'll use to begin paying off the loans. After I've advanced in my career, say after four or five years, **I expect to have started** earning enough so that 10% of my salary will amount to more money. **I really hope to have paid back** all my loans by the time I turn thirty.

Sara Williams, 21
Detroit, USA

B **MAKE PERSONAL COMPARISONS** Discuss the questions.

1 How are you similar to or different from any of the people in the Grammar Spotlight?

2 Do you cut back on your spending to buy something you want? Are you financially independent? Give specific examples from your own life.

DIGITAL INDUCTIVE ACTIVITY

C **GRAMMAR** COMPLETED FUTURE ACTIONS AND PLANS: THE FUTURE PERFECT AND PERFECT INFINITIVES

Use the future perfect to indicate an action that will be completed by a specified time in the future. It's common to state the particular time somewhere in the sentence. Form the future perfect with <u>will have</u> or <u>won't have</u> + a past participle. You can contract <u>will</u>.

By the time Cleo gets her visa, she **will have waited** for two years.
I'll have finished paying for my car before the end of the year.
They **won't have eaten** lunch before 2:00.
Will she **have finished** work by 9:00? (Yes, she will. / No, she won't.)

Use a perfect infinitive after <u>hope</u>, <u>expect</u>, <u>intend</u>, or <u>plan</u> to indicate that an action will or might take place before a specified time in the future. Form the perfect infinitive with <u>to have</u> + past participle.

By this time next year, I **plan to have saved** enough cash to buy a car.
They **intend to have completed** their studies by June 10th.
Do you **expect to have paid back** your loans in the next year? (Yes, I do. / No, I don't.)

Note: These are some expressions that commonly accompany statements in the future perfect:
before / after [May 15]
on / by [Tuesday]
by the time [she arrives]
in the next [month]

GRAMMAR BOOSTER p. 130
• The future continuous
• The future perfect continuous

DIGITAL
MORE
EXERCISES

D **NOTICE THE GRAMMAR** Find a statement in Spotlight on page 27 with the future perfect.

E **GRAMMAR PRACTICE** On a separate sheet of paper, use the cues to write sentences with the future perfect.

1 By the end of this month / I / put half my paycheck in the bank.

2 By next summer / Stan / save enough to make a down payment on an apartment.

3 Do you think you / lower / your credit card debt by December?

4 When / they / start / spending less than they earn?

F **GRAMMAR PRACTICE** Complete the paragraph, using perfect infinitives.

Ed Compton has been drowning in debt, so he has some emergency short-term goals.

By the end of the month, he .... a realistic budget that he can stick to.

1 intend / create

As a matter of fact, he .... the last payment on his car loan by October 30th.

2 hope / made

In addition, he .... saving 10% of his paycheck even before that. If he can stick to his

3 plan / begin

budget and savings plan, Mr. Compton .... all the money he owes within the year.

4 expect / pay back

G **ERROR CORRECTION** These sentences all have errors. On a separate sheet of paper, rewrite them correctly.

1 I expect to will earn enough money to buy a car by the end of the year.

2 Before they come back home, they will to have spent all the money they took with them.

3 We hope having completed our driver training by the end of the week.

4 By the time I'm thirty I will to be married for five years.

> **PRONUNCIATION BOOSTER** p. 143
> Sentence rhythm: thought groups

NOW YOU CAN Talk about financial goals and plans

A **NOTEPADDING** Write your short-term and long-term financial goals.

short-term goals	completion dates	long-term goals	completion dates
buy a racing bike	by this time next year	buy a house	by the time I'm thirty

short-term goals	completion dates	long-term goals	completion dates

DIGITAL VIDEO

B **DISCUSSION ACTIVATOR** Discuss your financial goals with a partner, using information from your notepad. Make statements in the future perfect and statements with <u>hope</u>, <u>expect</u>, <u>plan</u>, and <u>intend</u> with perfect infinitives. Say as much as you can. Be sure to change roles and then partners.

> ❝A year from now I'll have paid back my loans. ❞

> ❝By the time I graduate, I hope to have saved enough to buy a new car. ❞

Ideas
- be financially independent
- be out of debt
- cut back on spending
- create a realistic budget
- stick to a budget
- start saving money

GOAL Discuss good and bad money management

DIGITAL STRATEGIES **A** ▶ 2:09 **LISTENING WARM-UP** **VOCABULARY** **GOOD AND BAD MONEY MANAGEMENT**

Read and listen. Then listen again and repeat.

Good money management

I live within my means.

I keep track of my expenses.

I save regularly.

I always pay my credit card bills in full.

Bad money management

I live beyond my means.

I don't know where the money goes.

I live paycheck to paycheck.

I'm drowning in debt.

B **VOCABULARY PRACTICE** Complete each statement about money management, using the Vocabulary. Use each expression only once.

1 Some people say Mr. and Mrs. Strong are thrifty. They don't spend too much, and they always have money in the bank for a rainy day.

Mr. and Mrs. Strong ...*save regularly.*..

2 Andrew earns a small salary, but he's a big spender, so he's always out of cash.

Andrew ....

3 The Wilsons spend everything they earn and have almost no savings in the bank.

The Wilsons ....

4 When Katherine's credit card statement comes each month, she writes a check for the full balance.

Katherine ....

5 Sam acts as if he thinks money grows on trees. He can't remember where he spent this week's allowance.

Sam ....

6 Every month, Melanie pays a lot of interest and a late fee on her credit card bill. She can't sleep at night because of all that debt.

Melanie ....

7 Martha and Bill have everything they need and never spend more than they earn.

Martha and Bill ....

8 Sally always knows where her money goes. Every day she writes down everything she has bought.

Sally ....

C ▶ 2:10 **LISTEN TO CONFIRM CONTENT** Listen to three calls to a radio financial adviser. Check one or more suggestions the host gives each caller.

Caller 1	Caller 2	Caller 3
☐ **1** Save all your loose change.	☐ **1** Avoid impulse items.	☐ **1** Use only one or two cards.
☐ **2** Take money out of the ATM.	☐ **2** Talk to your parents.	☐ **2** Pay each month's bill in full.
☐ **3** Put money in the bank.	☐ **3** Save some money.	☐ **3** Stop using credit cards.
☐ **4** Stick to a budget.	☐ **4** Don't complain.	☐ **4** Stick to a budget.

D ▶ 2:11 **LISTEN TO SUMMARIZE** Listen again. On a separate sheet of paper, write a summary in two sentences of the reason each caller called the radio program.

E ▶ 2:12 **LISTEN TO EVALUATE** Choose one of the callers. Explain to a partner why you think Mack's advice is good or not. If so, add another suggestion. If not, offer your own advice.

NOW YOU CAN   Discuss good and bad money management

A **FRAME YOUR IDEAS** Analyze your own money management style. Choose the statements on the survey that best apply to you.

○ I live within my means.	○ I live beyond my means.
○ I keep track of my expenses.	○ I don't know where the money goes.
○ I save regularly.	○ I live from paycheck to paycheck and spend it all.
○ I always pay my credit card bills in full.	○ I'm drowning in debt.

B **PAIR WORK** Compare your answers on the survey. Do you have the same money management style? Explain the reasons for your choices and give real-life examples. Use the Vocabulary.

RECYCLE THIS LANGUAGE
- a big spender
- a cheapskate
- an impulse item
- stick to a budget
- save for a rainy day
- chip in
- way over my budget

GOAL Explain reasons for charitable giving

A READING WARM-UP What are some reasons people donate money to or volunteer for charities?

B ▶2:13 READING Read about some charities. How would you describe what a charity is?

HOME NEWS CHARITIES CONTACT US

CHARITIES OF THE WEEK

The following non-governmental, non-profit organizations have been among the most popular charities supported by both philanthropists and other generous people over the past year. Both of them have excellent reputations and both have been shown to use a high percentage of their funds for their work rather than for administrative expenses. They both seek contributions, and you can donate to each one through its website. If you are interested in volunteering your time, information about that can be found on the websites as well.

DOCTORS WITHOUT BORDERS

This well-known charitable organization dates from 1971, when 300 doctors, nurses,  and other staff, including journalists, officially formed it. Originally named (in French) Médecins Sans Frontières (MSF), it became known internationally in English as Doctors Without Borders. MSF's founding belief is that medical care should be available to everyone, regardless of location. Every year MSF provides emergency care to millions of people caught in crises in some 70 countries around the world. It offers assistance when catastrophic events such as armed conflicts, epidemics, malnutrition, or natural disasters overwhelm health resources. MSF also assists people who are neglected by their local health systems or who are otherwise excluded from medical care.

MSF medical personnel wear protective gear to avoid getting Ebola

CORAL REEF ALLIANCE

Pollution, overfishing, and rapid development are threatening coral reefs around the world. The guiding belief of the Coral Reef Alliance is that since these problems are caused by humans, they can be solved by humans. Corals are resilient to change, but if subjected to current levels of stress, they are in danger of extinction within a few decades. Coral Reef Alliance volunteers work in partnership with the people and groups who depend on reefs for their survival. They employ a three-pronged approach: reducing threats such as overfishing and poor water quality; helping communities benefit socially, culturally, and economically from conservation; and working directly with the tourism industry to decrease its environmental footprint. If the Coral Reef Alliance is successful, we will be able to enjoy beautiful coral reefs for a long time to come.

CORAL REEF ALLIANCE

A healthy coral reef teeming with fish

C WORD STUDY PARTS OF SPEECH Write the noun, adjective, or verb form of each of these words used in the Reading. Use a dictionary if necessary.

noun: charity	adjective:	verb: assist	noun: ....
noun: contribution	verb:	noun: pollution	verb: ....
verb: volunteer	noun:	noun: threat	verb: ....
verb: donate	noun:	noun: extinction	adjective: ....

D UNDERSTAND MEANING FROM CONTEXT Complete the statements about information in the Reading with a word from Exercise C.

1 Poor water quality is a .... to healthy coral reefs.

2 .... from the Coral Reef Alliance help communities conserve the health of their coral reefs.

3 If we don't improve the environment, coral reefs may face .... within a few years.

4 MSF provides emergency medical .... when there aren't enough local resources.

5 Tourism has contributed to the .... of the water around coral reefs.

6 The .... of philanthropists and others are welcomed by MSF and the Coral Reef Alliance.

E **DRAW CONCLUSIONS**   Complete each statement with the most likely conclusion, based on the Reading.

1 The purpose of the Charities of the Week column is ....

  a to tell readers which charities they should volunteer for

  b to educate the public each week about some good charities

2 The medical personnel of MSF usually ....

  a travel to places where they are needed

  b assist the people mostly in the countries where the medical personnel live

3 The people helped by the Coral Reef alliance are probably ....

  a people who fish for a living near coral reefs

  b tourists who visit areas with coral reefs

DIGITAL EXTRA CHALLENGE **F** **EXPRESS AND SUPPORT AN OPINION**   Which of the two charities does more important work? Explain your opinion.

NOW YOU CAN   Explain reasons for charitable giving

A **FRAME YOUR IDEAS**   Write a checkmark next to people or organizations you would contribute to. Write an X next to the ones you wouldn't. Then tell your partner your reasons.

a homeless person
an organization that helps the homeless
a disaster relief agency
an animal protection agency

a school in a poor neighborhood
a museum
a religious institution
other

> " I'd contribute to an animal protection agency. I think it's our responsibility to protect animals. "

B **PAIR WORK**   First rate the reasons you think people donate money to charities from 1 to 8, with 1 being the best reason. Compare and discuss your ratings with a partner.

..... to change society
..... so people will admire them
..... to be a good example
..... so people will thank them
..... for religious reasons
..... to feel good
..... to help others
..... other

DIGITAL SPEAKING BOOSTER **C** **DISCUSSION**   Put together the information from Exercises A and B. Discuss your general and specific reasons for contributing to the charities you checked, saying as much as you can. Use words from Word Study when possible.

> " My motivation for contributing to charity is mostly to help other people. That's the reason I give money to homeless people and organizations that help the homeless. "

OPTIONAL WRITING   Choose a charity. Write a paragraph explaining why people should donate or volunteer for this cause. Present your ideas to your class or group.

WRITING Organizing information by degrees of importance

A **WRITING SKILL** Study the rules.

When writing a paragraph, organize your ideas and sentences logically. Use words and phrases to indicate to the reader the relative importance of the ideas. Write the ideas in order of importance, starting with the most important. Notice the commas.

First, in order of importance,
Most importantly,
To begin with,

Secondly, / Thirdly, etc.
Following that,
After that,

Finally,
Last but not least,
Least importantly,
As a final point,

WRITING MODEL

I am proud to say that I am financially independent. My friends occasionally ask me how I did it and ask me to give them advice. I like to say, "You have to be financially intelligent." How? **First and most importantly**, spend less than you earn. One way to do that is to create a budget and stick to it. **Secondly**, don't charge things on credit cards that you can't pay for at the end of the month. **Last but not least**, put a little money into savings whenever you can.

B **PRACTICE** Complete the paragraph with words and phrases indicating order of importance.

I try to be generous to those in need and always contribute a portion of my income to charities that I think are worthwhile. Since I don't have a lot of money, I have to consider where my money can do the most good. There are several issues I need to think about before sending money. .... , I want to know if the charity is financially sound; that is, does most of the money it receives actually go to the people in need? Or does it spend too much money on salaries for employees of the organization? I get this information from Charity Navigator on the Internet. .... , although nearly as important to me, is does the charity address a crisis of some sort, such as an epidemic? There are so many worthy charities, but to me, the ones that provide immediate help that can prevent death are the most important. .... , I always ask if the charity provides help to all people, regardless of who they are. I don't care if the people I help are in my country or some other country, and I don't care about their religion, race, or nationality.

C **APPLY THE WRITING SKILL** Write a one-paragraph personal statement for a job or university application. Describe three ways you manage your financial responsibilities. Use vocabulary from this unit and organize your ideas in order of importance. Provide examples to support your claims.

SELF-CHECK

- [ ] Did I present my ideas in order of importance?
- [ ] Did I use the words and phrases to indicate their relative importance?
- [ ] Did I use correct punctuation?

36   UNIT 3

A ▶2:14 Listen to the conversations. Then write the letter of the statement that best summarizes each conversation. Listen again if necessary.

   a He should be more thrifty.

   b He's not really a big spender. He's just feeling generous today.

   c If he'd known it would be so hard to put together, he never would have bought it.

Conversation 1 ......   Conversation 2 ......   Conversation 3 ......

B Complete the statements about bad money management, using four different phrases from the Vocabulary in Lesson 3.

   1 Marian Bates receives her salary on the last Friday of every month. By the end of the next month, she has no money left. She ....

   2 Paul and Clare Oliver never pay their credit cards in full, and every month the balance on their card is bigger. They're ....

   3 Cheryl spends more than she earns. She ....

   4 Eleanor's mother gives her money every week for transportation to and from school, but by Thursday the money's gone. Eleanor ....

C Complete each statement with true information, using the future perfect or a perfect infinitive.

   1 By this weekend, ...

   2 At the end of this school year, I intend ....

   3 By the time I retire ....

   4 By the year 2020, I hope ....

   5 Before I leave this English program, I expect ....

D On a separate sheet of paper, answer each question using <u>wish</u> and the past perfect or <u>should have</u> and a past participle to express a true regret from the past.

   1 What do you wish you had done differently in your life? ....
   ....

   2 What decision should you have made that you didn't? ....
   ....

E Explain in your own words the meaning of the following words and phrases.

   1 financially independent: ....

   2 a budget: ....

   3 a short-term goal ....

   4 a long-term goal ....

   5 astronomical ....

   6 a loan ....

TEST-TAKING SKILLS BOOSTER p. 153

Web Project: Charities
www.english.com/summit3e

COMMUNICATION GOALS

1 Describe clothing details and formality
2 Talk about changes in clothing customs
3 Examine questionable cosmetic procedures
4 Discuss appearance and self-esteem

PREVIEW

A FRAME YOUR IDEAS Match each quotation with the person or people you think most likely said it.

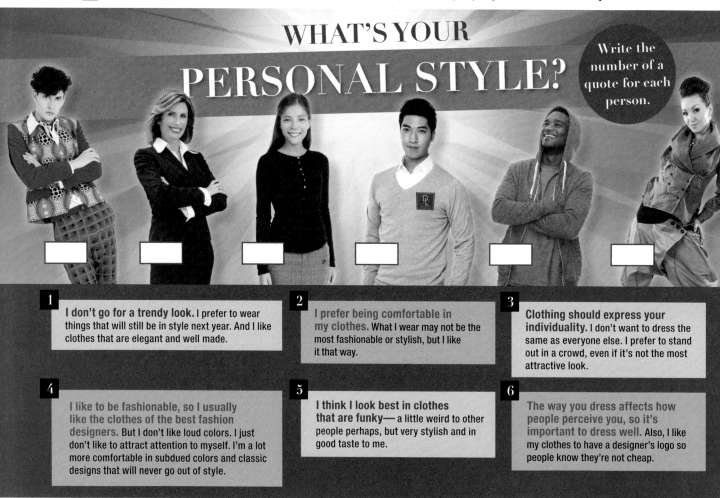

WHAT'S YOUR
PERSONAL STYLE?

Write the number of a quote for each person.

1 I don't go for a trendy look. I prefer to wear things that will still be in style next year. And I like clothes that are elegant and well made.

2 I prefer being comfortable in my clothes. What I wear may not be the most fashionable or stylish, but I like it that way.

3 Clothing should express your individuality. I don't want to dress the same as everyone else. I prefer to stand out in a crowd, even if it's not the most attractive look.

4 I like to be fashionable, so I usually like the clothes of the best fashion designers. But I don't like loud colors. I just don't like to attract attention to myself. I'm a lot more comfortable in subdued colors and classic designs that will never go out of style.

5 I think I look best in clothes that are funky— a little weird to other people perhaps, but very stylish and in good taste to me.

6 The way you dress affects how people perceive you, so it's important to dress well. Also, I like my clothes to have a designer's logo so people know they're not cheap.

B ▶ 2:15 VOCABULARY   ADJECTIVES TO DESCRIBE FASHION   Listen and repeat.

		Don't forget
fashionable / stylish	representing a style being worn by many people who dress well	wild
funky	modern and attractive, but in an unconventional way	conservative
trendy	a temporarily popular style that probably won't last	modest
classic	an unchanging style that is always fashionable	appropriate
elegant	beautiful and of high quality	inappropriate
subdued	(of colors) not too bright or too colorful	casual
loud	(of colors) very bright and too attention-getting	formal
		informal

C DISCUSSION   Describe the outfit of each person in the photos above, using one or more of the adjectives from the Vocabulary. Explain, using examples.

D ▶ 2:16 **SPOTLIGHT**   Read a conversation between two travelers in an airport duty-free shop. Notice the spotlighted language.

Karen: Roya, could I get your opinion on something?

Roya: Sure. What's up?

Karen: What do you think of these pants? For a teenager, I mean. Not for me.

Roya: The ones with the sequins on the bottom? A bit flashy, don't you think? I think they'd **attract too much attention**, know what I'm saying?

Karen: Funny. To me they're kind of cute, maybe a little funky—but not **over the top**. At least not where I come from.

Roya: Well, it may just be a cultural thing, but in my country, no girl from a nice family **would be caught dead** wearing something as immodest as that. In fact, her parents would never even let her buy them.

Karen: Interesting . . . But you must be right. This has got to be cultural. In the U.S., no one would even **give them a second thought**. If they had a bunch of holes in them, I'd agree that they were in bad taste.

Roya: But they draw attention to a part of the body you don't want people staring at, right?

Karen: Well, come to think of it, **you have a point**. But personally, I think the jeans are pretty cute. I guess customs are different everywhere.

Roya: It's not that I think girls and women should always wear frumpy,* baggy clothes. But people can be modern and fashionable and still show some self-respect.

*frumpy = old-fashioned, loose (only used for women's clothes)

E **UNDERSTAND IDIOMS AND EXPRESSIONS**   Paraphrase these quotations from Spotlight.

1 "I think they'd attract too much attention."

> ❝ I think they might make too many people look at the person wearing them. ❞

2 "… but not over the top."

3 "No girl … would be caught dead wearing something as immodest as that."

4 "… no one would even give them a second thought."

5 "… you have a point."

F **THINK AND EXPLAIN**   Discuss these questions.

1 In what way do Karen and Roya's perspectives on good and bad taste differ?

2 Whose opinion represents the opinion of a majority of people in your country?

SPEAKING

A **PAIR WORK**   Read the quotations and sayings about the significance of clothes. Then work with a partner to paraphrase them. Think of sayings in your own language that express similar ideas.

❝ **FASHIONS** FADE; STYLE IS **ETERNAL.** ❞
Yves Saint-Laurent
French fashion designer

❝ SO SOON AS A **FASHION** IS **UNIVERSAL,** IT IS OUT OF DATE. ❞
Marie Von Ebner-Eschenbach
Austrian writer

❝ **FASHION DESIGNERS** ARE DICTATORS OF **TASTE.** ❞
Karl Lagerfeld
German fashion designer

❝ DON'T BE INTO **TRENDS.** DON'T MAKE **FASHION** OWN YOU, BUT YOU DECIDE WHAT YOU ARE—WHAT **YOU** WANT TO **EXPRESS** BY THE WAY **YOU** DRESS AND THE WAY **YOU** LIVE. ❞
Gianni Versace
Italian fashion designer

❝ WHOEVER SAID THAT MONEY CAN'T BUY **HAPPINESS** SIMPLY DIDN'T KNOW WHERE TO GO **SHOPPING.** ❞
Bo Derek
American actor and model

B **DISCUSSION**   What, in your opinion, do our clothes tell others about us?

GOAL Describe clothing details and formality

DIGITAL STRATEGIES **A** ▶2:17 **VOCABULARY** **DESCRIBING CLOTHES**
Read and listen.

▶2:18 **Adjectives**
long-sleeved
low-cut
print
striped
plaid
short-sleeved
solid

I've got on a **long-sleeved cocktail dress**. A bit **low-cut**, but appropriate… . What color? Actually, it's a black-and-white **print**.

▶2:19 **Formal clothes**
a cocktail dress
a dress shirt
an evening gown
a tuxedo

Don't forget
Informal clothes
V-neck
crewneck
turtleneck
sweater
polo shirt
jeans
T-shirt
blazer
cardigan

You should see my costume for the play! I'm wearing a nice **dress shirt**—like for the office. But I'm also wearing **striped** shorts and carrying a **plaid** jacket! Ridiculous and in terrible taste, but great!

Hi, Mom … Dan and I are on our way to the charity ball. It's formal, so I've got on a **short-sleeved evening gown** in a great **solid** dark purple **color**. Dan's got on a **tuxedo**. I'll send you a selfie!

B ▶2:20 **LISTEN FOR DETAILS** Listen to the conversations. Circle the letter of the illustration that answers each question.

1 Which man are they talking about?

a   b   c

2 Which girl are they discussing?

a   b   c

3 Which dress are they describing?

a   b   c

4 Which shirt will he buy?

a   b   c

C **PAIR WORK** Take turns describing the clothes in Exercise B. Your partner says which clothes you are describing. Use the Vocabulary.

PRONUNCIATION BOOSTER   p. 143

Linking sounds

D APPLY THE VOCABULARY With a partner, discuss your opinions about these fashions. Use the Vocabulary and other adjectives you know to describe the clothing details.

> 𝟨𝟨 I love the long-sleeved solid black dress. I think it's classic and elegant and would look great anywhere. 𝟫𝟫

NOW YOU CAN Describe clothing details and formality

A ▶ 2:21 CONVERSATION SPOTLIGHT Read and listen. Notice the spotlighted conversation strategies.

A: **Can I ask you a question about** the reception this weekend?
B: Sure. What would you like to know?
A: How formal will it be? **I mean,** what kind of clothes are we expected to wear?
B: **Actually,** it'll be pretty formal, I think.
A: **So** would a nice long-sleeved blouse and a pair of black dress pants be OK?
B: **I think that might be** a little underdressed. Most women will probably wear cocktail dresses.
A: Great! I've got a beautiful cocktail dress I can wear.

Formality
underdressed
overdressed

B ▶ 2:22 RHYTHM AND INTONATION Listen again and repeat. Then practice the conversation with a partner.

C CONVERSATION ACTIVATOR Create a similar conversation about formality at a different kind of event. Ask about specific clothes, using clothing and adjectives from the Vocabulary. Start like this: *Can I ask you a question about...?* Be sure to change roles and then partners.

DIGITAL VIDEO
DIGITAL SPEAKING BOOSTER

DON'T STOP!
• Ask more questions about the event.
• Provide details about the clothes.
• Make a decision about what to wear.
• Say as much as you can.

RECYCLE THIS LANGUAGE	
· trendy	· subdued
· funky	· loud
· frumpy	· flashy
· classic	· in good taste
· elegant	· in bad taste

OPTIONAL WRITING Write about a real or invented event when someone was underdressed (or overdressed). Use the Vocabulary.

A ▶ 2:23 **GRAMMAR SPOTLIGHT** Read the article. Notice the spotlighted grammar.

Dressing up and Dressing down

Walk around any urban business district in the U.S., and you'll see **a majority of** office workers in "business casual" attire. Only **a few** will be wearing the more formal suits, skirts, and dresses seen in more conservative locations around the world. Business casual style developed in several steps, **most** people say, in the U.S. state of Hawaii. Here's **a little** history:

In 1966, the Hawaiian clothing industry was trying to sell **more** Hawaiian, or "aloha," shirts. The industry encouraged Hawaiian businesses to let their employees wear these colorful print shirts to the office one day a week, on Fridays. But the style became so popular that by 1970 it had become standard dress **all** days of the week there.

The trend spread to the state of California, which has always had **less** office formality than the rest of the country. There, people called the trend "casual Friday." Later, in the 1990s, the concept got more of a boost, again by the clothing industry. It was during that time that **a number of** companies began promoting casual khaki pants. **Lots of** ads showed both men and women wearing them with dress shirts and blazers or sweaters. This look quickly became the new office standard.

Some wish the pendulum would swing back towards a more traditional, elegant look, but **plenty of** other people say this is unlikely. In fact, **more and more** companies, particularly in the creative and technology sectors, now permit jeans and even T-shirts in the office. **Many** younger people are used to this look and would resist going back to more conservative office dress.

B **EXAMINE CULTURAL EXPECTATIONS** Discuss the questions.

1 Can clothing affect people's work quality and productivity in offices? How?

2 What should the limits of formality be in office dress? Be specific.

C **GRAMMAR** **QUANTIFIERS: REVIEW AND EXPANSION**
DIGITAL INDUCTIVE ACTIVITY

Some quantifiers can only be used with singular count nouns.

one shoe	**each** man	**every** friend

Some quantifiers can only be used with plural count nouns.

a few sports	**both** stores	**a pair of** shoes
many workers	**several** men	**a number of** trends
a couple of skirts	**at least** three	**a majority of** tuxedos

Some quantifiers can only be used with non-count nouns.

a little formality	**much** choice	**a great deal** of conflict
less fun	**not as much** formality	**a great amount of** interest

> **Note:** The quantifier a majority of can also be used with singular count nouns that include more than one person. Use a third-person singular verb.
>
> A majority of **the class thinks** shorts are inappropriate for school.
>
> A majority of **the population prefers** casual clothes in the office.

Some quantifiers can be used with *both* count and non-count nouns.

Count nouns	Non-count nouns
no people	**no** choice
some / **any** cocktail dresses	**some** / **any** fashion
a lot of / **lots of** windbreakers	**a lot of** / **lots of** style
a third of the offices	**a third of** the money
plenty of young men	**plenty of** interest
most clothes	**most** criticism
all young people	**all** fashion
more evening gowns	**more** music
more and more women	**more and more** clothing

> **GRAMMAR BOOSTER** p. 131
> • Quantifiers: <u>a few</u> and <u>few</u>; <u>a little</u> and <u>little</u>
> • Quantifiers: using <u>of</u>
> • Quantifiers used without referents
> • Subject-verb agreement of quantifiers followed by <u>of</u>

D **UNDERSTAND THE GRAMMAR**   Circle the correct quantifier. Explain your answer.

1 (Most / Much) men and women today like having a wide choice of clothes to wear.

2 (A number of / A great deal of) stores in this mall sell trendy clothes.

3 (All / Every) guest at the dinner wore formal clothing.

4 A more liberal dress code has resulted in (less / fewer) choices in formal clothing.

5 Seventy-five years ago, there were (a little / a few) stores that sold women's pants.

> 66 **Much** can't be used with count nouns. 99

E **GRAMMAR PRACTICE**   Circle the letters of *all* the quantifiers that can complete each sentence correctly. Explain your answer, based on the grammar chart.

1 If people go to ...... formal events, they need appropriate clothes.
   a a lot of   **b** several   **c** a number of   **d** a great deal of

2 ...... children don't think much about what clothes to wear.
   a most   **b** a great deal of   **c** every   **d** a majority of

3 Since the invitation doesn't specify the level of formality, it's clear that ...... person needs to decide on his or her own what to wear.
   a some   **b** each   **c** every   **d** most

4 There are ...... tailors who can make anything you buy look great on you.
   a a number of   **b** a few   **c** plenty of   **d** a little

5 I was surprised to read that ...... women didn't wear pants 50 years ago.
   a a lot of   **b** some   **c** every   **d** less

> 66 **A great deal of** can only be used with non-count nouns. 99

NOW YOU CAN   Talk about changes in clothing customs

A **NOTEPADDING**   Contrast what you imagine young people wore 100 years ago with what they wear today.

Event	100 years ago	Today
a walk in the park		
a formal reception or wedding		
dinner at a nice restaurant		
dinner at a friend's home		
a party at school or in the office		

B **SUMMARIZE**   In a group, compare your classmates' ideas. Use quantifiers to summarize your classmates' ideas.

> 66 A majority of the class said they thought ... 99

> 66 A few students said ... 99

C **DISCUSSION ACTIVATOR**   How much would you say clothing trends have changed in your country? Describe how they have changed. Use the information from your notepad. Say as much as you can.

> 66 In the old days, everyone wore pretty formal clothes to a dinner in a nice restaurant, but today fewer people do. 99

43

A **READING WARM-UP** Are there any cosmetic procedures you think should be illegal? Explain.

B ▶ 2:24 **READING** Read about fish pedicures. In what ways is this treatment risky?

Questionable
COSMETIC TREATMENTS

In this wide world, there's always someone ready to shell out money for a treatment that promises results.

Is it safe to let *Garra rufa* fish, or "doctor fish," exfoliate your feet in a fish spa pedicure, eating away quantities of dead skin and leaving your feet looking sandal-ready? Although fish pedicures are popular in many parts of the world, the governments of a number of U.S. states and at least two Canadian provinces have banned the practice, making it illegal to provide this service. Although some experts say there is not much of a serious risk to health, and although no actual illnesses have been caused by this procedure, most bans are based on one or more of the following reasons:

Since the fish remain in the pedicure tubs, it's impossible to clean them between clients. Bacteria and other pathogens can build up in the water, and if a client has a cut or break in the skin, these organisms can enter and cause infection. In fact, New York dermatologist Dr. Riya Prasad says, "Today there are so many antibiotic-resistant bacteria that I advise my patients to walk the other way when they see a salon or spa offering these pedicures. Better safe than sorry!"

The fish themselves cannot be disinfected or sanitized to prevent them from spreading bacteria. Due to the cost of the fish, salon owners are likely to use the same fish multiple times with different clients, which increases the risk of spreading infection.

Chinchin, a species often mislabeled as *Garra rufa* and used in pedicures, grows teeth and can break the skin, further increasing the risk. *Garra rufa*, on the other hand, are toothless.

According to the U.S. Fish and Wildlife Service, *Garra rufa* could pose a threat to native plant and animal life if released into the wild in places where it isn't native. Non-native species can reproduce without limit because there may be few natural predators to kill them and control their numbers.

And in addition to the harm these pedicures can do to the environment and human health, the fish at a salon or spa must be contained in an aquarium with no natural food source and depend on human skin to survive. In order to get the fish to eat the skin on a client's feet, they must be starved, and this could be considered animal cruelty, which is illegal in many places.

The preponderance of evidence leads one to believe that fish pedicures are doubtful at best and dangerous at worst. And public opinion seems to be building against them, with city after city making them illegal.

> Fish pedicures? Yuck and double yuck! Just get a nice clean pedicure from a licensed cosmetician. If the hygiene argument doesn't convince you, just think how terrible the experience is for the poor little fishies!
> –Minnie Edwards, biology teacher

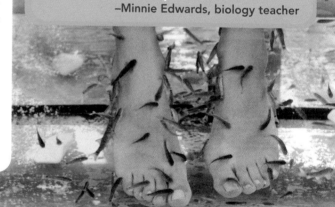

C **UNDERSTAND MEANING FROM CONTEXT** Complete the statements with words from the box.

1 When someone uses something to .... your feet, he or she removes dead skin.

2 Another way to say that a government doesn't permit something is to say it .... it.

3 .... are pathogenic organisms that can grow in water.

4 When you .... something, you clean it to remove harmful organisms.

5 When you .... something, it means that you give it the wrong name.

6 A .... is an animal that kills and eats other animals.

| bacteria |
| bans |
| disinfect |
| exfoliate |
| mislabel |
| predator |

1 Where can you get a fish pedicure?
  a In many countries around the world.   **b** In all the U.S. states and Canadian provinces.

2 What is one reason that fish pedicures aren't permitted in some places?
  a They have caused serious illnesses.   **b** They can cause infection.

3 Where can bacteria enter a client's skin?
  a In the fish's mouth.   **b** In a cut in the client's skin.

4 What makes chinchin more dangerous than garrra rufa?
  a They can reproduce in the wild.
  b They have teeth that can break the client's skin, which can cause infection.

5 What would salon owners have to do to keep the water free of pathogens?
  a They would have to wash the tank and change the fish after each pedicure.
  b They would have to clean each client's feet.

6 Why do some people consider the treatment of pedicure fish cruel?
  a Because in order to get them to eat skin, they have to be starved.
  b Because keeping them in aquariums is unsanitary and can cause infection.

DIGITAL EXTRA CHALLENGE **E EXPRESS AND SUPPORT AN OPINION** Discuss with a partner. Would you consider getting a fish pedicure? Explain your reasons.

NOW YOU CAN Examine questionable cosmetic procedures

A FRAME YOUR IDEAS Read the ads and rate them. Discuss your ratings and reasons with a partner.

Ratings.
✓ = Looks good to me.
? = I'd have to know more.
✗ = I wouldn't try it even if you paid me!

Face-Slapping **Massage ... Based on science!**

Rejuvenate your aging face with the ancient practice of face-slapping. Based on scientifically proven physical tapping known as "tapotement" and used extensively in Swedish massage, both gentle and more aggressive slaps with a flat or cupped palm improve circulation and reduce the appearance of wrinkles, resulting in a more youthful appearance.

My rating ☐

The Swiss Chocolate Mud Wrap is a "sweet experience."

Swiss Chocolate Mud Wrap

Soak in the luxury of the finest Swiss chocolate mixed with sticky Mississippi River mud—the ultimate full-body mask to hydrate your skin, slim your silhouette, and stimulate your circulation all at once. Effects are achieved by the natural essential oils in the chocolate that are released as the mud dries and contracts. Emerge from a series of three treatments a newer, smoother, slimmer you.

My rating ☐

Tapeworm Express Diet*

Don't knock it if you haven't tried it! Under a doctor's supervision, you simply swallow a small pill. Within days, one or more tapeworms will absorb all the food you eat, resulting in extra-fast weight loss. Once you have reached your ideal weight, the doctor will administer an anti-parasite pill, killing the tapeworm, which will pass out of your body harmlessly.

"I tried this diet and reached my ideal weight fast!"

* Only for healthy individuals. The tapeworm express diet can cause abdominal complications, meningitis, and dementia.

My rating ☐

B DISCUSSION What specific dangerous or harmful procedures have you seen or heard about? What can or should be done about them?

RECYCLE THIS LANGUAGE
· It's just a matter of time until ...
· I mean, what are you going to do?
· It is what it is.
· Better safe than sorry.
· Can I ask you a question?

A ▶2:25 **LISTENING WARM-UP WORD STUDY: COMPOUND WORDS WITH SELF-** Study the words. Then use a dictionary to find two more nouns and two more adjectives with the prefix self-.

NOUNS

self-confidence the belief that one has the ability to do things well
Parents can build their children's self-confidence by helping them develop their talents and abilities.

self-esteem the attitude of acceptance and approval of oneself
High self-esteem can help a person succeed, and low self-esteem can be damaging.

self-image the opinion one has about one's own abilities, appearance, and character
A person's self-image is often formed very early in life.

self-pity the feeling of being sorry for oneself
When you feel that life is unfair and that others have treated you poorly, it's not unusual to feel self-pity.

ADJECTIVES

self-centered interested only in oneself
Children are naturally self-centered, but they usually learn to be more interested in others as they grow up.

self-confident believing that one has the ability to do things well; not shy or nervous in social situations
Janet is a very self-confident young woman. She'll do well at the university.

self-conscious worried about what one looks like or what other people think of one's appearance
Everyone at the meeting was dressed casually, so I felt self-conscious in my suit.

self-critical tending to find fault with oneself
Paul is too self-critical. He always focuses on his mistakes rather than his accomplishments.

B **WORD STUDY PRACTICE** Complete each statement, using one of the compound words with self-.

1 Eleanor Ricci entered the auditorium with her usual .... and began her presentation.

2 Even though my brother Martin always wears great clothes, he feels .... and usually asks me to tell him if he looks OK.

3 They say that children's .... is built by receiving parental praise for their accomplishments.

4 A positive .... can help people through the difficulties of life without feeling like failures when things go wrong.

5 People who spend a lot of time talking about themselves are ....

6 I don't know why Paul is so .... He's great at everything and more successful than almost everyone else.

7 We tried to encourage Sylvie to look on the bright side, but after she lost her job, she just couldn't stop wallowing in ....

8 .... people don't just sit around worrying about not being able to do things. They try their best and assume their best is good enough.

 C ▶2:26 **LISTEN FOR MAIN IDEAS** Listen to a university lecture. Then read the statements and choose the one that expresses the main idea of the lecture.

☐ 1 Female self-image is heavily influenced by messages in the media.

☐ 2 Many fashion models today are super-thin.

☐ 3 Eighty per cent of ten-year-olds are on diets.

☐ 4 Anorexia is a common eating disorder.

Super-thin models are demanded by fashion designers, magazine editors, and advertisers.

D ▶2:27 **LISTEN FOR DETAILS** Read the following questions. Answer them, listening again if necessary.

1 What kind of body is currently in style?

2 What change has taken place in the look of fashion models over the last fifty years?

3 What is one serious consequence of feeling like you're fat all the time?

4 How can women help themselves overcome the negative messages in the media?

5 How can people help their daughters avoid a negative self-image?

E ▶2:28 **LISTEN TO SUMMARIZE** With a partner, write a summary statement about the lecture.

Photos are often altered to make models and actresses appear thinner than they are.

NOW YOU CAN Discuss appearance and self-esteem

A **FRAME YOUR IDEAS** Take the survey. Then compare ratings with a partner.

HOW MUCH DO YOU AGREE WITH EACH STATEMENT ABOUT MEN AND WOMEN IN YOUR COUNTRY?

STRONGLY DISAGREE ⟵   ⟶ STRONGLY AGREE

	1	2	3	4	5
1 Most women are self-conscious about their bodies.	1	2	3	4	5
2 Most men are self-conscious about their bodies.	1	2	3	4	5
3 Most women are self-conscious about their faces.	1	2	3	4	5
4 Most men are self-conscious about their faces.	1	2	3	4	5
5 Most women want to look more like women in the media.	1	2	3	4	5
6 Most men want to look more like men in the media.	1	2	3	4	5
7 Most women think women need to be beautiful.	1	2	3	4	5
8 Most men think women need to be beautiful.	1	2	3	4	5
9 Most women think men need to be handsome.	1	2	3	4	5
10 Most men think men need to be handsome.	1	2	3	4	5

B **NOTEPADDING** Make a list of positive and negative factors that affect self-esteem.

Build self-esteem	Harm self-esteem
Parental love	"Messages" in the media

Build self-esteem	Harm self-esteem

C **DISCUSSION**

DIGITAL SPEAKING BOOSTER

1 How can the positive factors you listed on your notepad be promoted?

2 Which of the negative factors on your notepad can be changed or corrected?

3 Do you think life is easier for people who are attractive? Explain your opinion.

4 In an ideal world, what should one's self-esteem be based on? Explain your opinion.

A **WRITING SKILL** Study the rules.

Compare Connecting words that show similarities	Contrast Connecting words that show differences
like **Like** Sylvia, I wear jeans all the time. OR I wear jeans all the time, **like** Sylvia.	**unlike** **Unlike** her sister, Wendy wears great clothes. OR Wendy wears great clothes, **unlike** her sister.

similarly
 	
I grew up paying little attention to fashion.
  Similarly, my brother was not very
  interested in clothes. OR
I grew up paying little attention to fashion;
  similarly, my brother was not very interested
  in clothes.
	in contrast
	
	I've always liked to wear black to evening events.
	  In contrast, my sister prefers white. OR
	I've always liked to wear black to evening events;
	  in contrast, my sister prefers white.

likewise
 	
My mother always liked elegant clothes.
  Likewise, her two sisters did, too. OR
My mother always liked elegant clothes;
  likewise, her two sisters did, too.
	however
	
	Lily had to wear a uniform when she was in
	  school. **However,** I was allowed to wear
	  anything I wanted. OR
	Lily had to wear a uniform when she was in
	  school; **however,** I was allowed to wear
	  anything I wanted.

as well / not either
 	
Many people spend too much money on clothes.
  Some spend too much on shoes **as well.**
Our parents' generation didn't worry so much
  about fashion. Their own parents **didn't
  either.**
	while / whereas
	
	Sam spends a lot of money on clothes **while**
	  (or **whereas**) Jeff rarely does. OR
	While (or **whereas**) Sam spends a lot of money
	  on clothes, Jeff rarely does.

B **PRACTICE** Read the paragraph, inserting logical connecting words for comparing and contrasting.

  My husband, Jack, generally appreciates fashion, but we don't always agree on clothes and what to wear. I like to shop in small boutiques; .... 1 , my husband also appreciates the attention a shopper gets in a small store. .... 2 , I always buy funky, trendy clothes. .... 3 , Jack is more conservative. And it won't be surprising for anyone to learn that .... 4 my husband, I tend to like loud colors and bold prints, ... 5 he prefers a more subdued look. .... 6 I feel self-confident that whatever I wear will be OK .... 7 Jack can be a little self-conscious and always tries to wear non-controversial clothes. But, as they say, "opposites attract," and we both like the way the other person dresses, even if our tastes for ourselves aren't the same.

 C **APPLY THE WRITING SKILL**
Choose a topic below. Write two paragraphs comparing and contrasting ideas. In your first paragraph, write about the differences. In your second paragraph, write about the similarities. Use connecting words and include a topic sentence for each paragraph.

Topics
- Compare and contrast your fashion style and tastes with those of someone you know.
- Compare and contrast fashion today with fashion five, ten, or twenty years ago.

SELF-CHECK
☐ Did I use connecting words for comparing?
☐ Did I use connecting words for contrasting?
☐ Does each paragraph have a topic sentence?

A ▶2:29 Listen to the conversations about fashion and style. Choose the adjective that best summarizes each speaker's point of view.

1 They think the purses in the magazine are ....
   a frumpy   b trendy   c flashy

2 He thinks the jacket Carl is wearing is ....
   a funky   b subdued   c loud

3 They think the girl's hair is ....
   a elegant   b in bad taste   c classic

4 The salesperson is suggesting that the dress is ....
   a elegant   b funky   c trendy

5 She thinks the blouse her friend is holding isn't ....
   a in bad taste   b stylish   c frumpy

B Complete each statement with an appropriate word or phrase.

1 A piece of clothing that's all one color is ....

2 A shirt with different color lines making square patterns is ....

3 A piece of clothing with vertical or horizontal lines in different colors is ....

4 A very formal suit a man might wear to a wedding or a reception is ....

5 A short, elegant dress for a party in the evening is ....

6 A long, very formal dress for a wedding or a reception is ....

7 When a person is wearing something much too informal for an occasion, he or she is ....

8 If a man comes to the office in a tuxedo, people will say that he's ....

9 Many people think that a dress or blouse that's .... is too revealing and in bad taste.

10 When it's cold outside, it's better to wear a .... shirt.

C Cross out the one quantifier that cannot be used in each sentence.

1 (Every / A few / Most) older people find flashy clothes in bad taste.

2 The company where I work says that it will permit us to come to the office in jeans (one / a couple of / a few) days a month.

3 (Most / Many / Every) young girls aren't worried about the way they look.

4 (Much / A majority of / A number of) parents are concerned about the effect the media has on young boys as well.

5 When my great-grandparents were young, (many / most / much) women wore only dresses.

6 I'd say your friends could use (some / a little / a few) fashion advice.

7 There are (several / most / many) reasons so many young women have eating disorders.

8 A new study says that (most / many / every) children who watch TV for more than six hours a day may have problems with self-esteem as teenagers.

D On a separate sheet of paper, write five sentences, each one using one of the quantifiers from the box.

several	a majority	few	little	more and more

Web Project: Trend Spotters
www.english.com/summit3e

UNIT 5

Communities

COMMUNICATION GOALS
1 Politely ask someone not to do something
2 Complain about public conduct
3 Suggest ways to avoid being a victim of urban crime
4 Discuss the meaning of community

PREVIEW

A **FRAME YOUR IDEAS** Complete the questionnaire about your ideal community. How closely do your answers describe where you live now? In what ways are they different?

Home	About	Questionnaires	Top stories		Search	🔍

Whether you're planning to move soon or just dreaming about your future, this questionnaire will help you focus on what's most important to you.

1. What kind of environment would you prefer to live in?

- ◯ a densely-populated urban area with skyscrapers
- ◯ a medium-sized urban area
- ◯ a suburb, just outside a city, with convenient transportation
- ◯ a small town in a rural area with a slower pace of life

2. Which of the following describe your ideal neighborhood?

- ◯ is near my school or job
- ◯ is peaceful and quiet
- ◯ is lively and bustling with activity
- ◯ is friendly, with people who say hello to each other
- ◯ has a mix of apartment buildings and private homes
- ◯ has mainly private homes
- ◯ has mainly modern high-rise apartment buildings
- ◯ has lots of well-maintained historical buildings
- ◯ is safe, with very little crime
- ◯ is very secure, with security cameras and guards
- ◯ other: [_____]

a rural town

an urban area

3. Which neighborhood amenities would you want easy access to?

- ◯ reliable public transportation
- ◯ a large modern mall
- ◯ a variety of small businesses, such as hair salons, dry cleaners, florists, etc.
- ◯ a large supermarket
- ◯ a market where you can buy fresh farm produce
- ◯ theaters and stadiums
- ◯ a hospital and clinics
- ◯ parks and fitness centers
- ◯ other: [_____]

B ▶ 3:01 **VOCABULARY** **TYPES OF LOCATIONS** Listen and repeat. Then, with a partner, write a definition for each of these location types.

> an urban area
> a rural area
> the suburbs

C **PAIR WORK** Compare your answers in the questionnaire to determine if you have the same preferences. Discuss and explain the reasons for your choices.

D ▶ 3:02 **SPOTLIGHT**   Read and listen to a conversation between two former colleagues. Notice the spotlighted language.

Bill: Hi, Luiz!

Luiz: Bill? What a surprise!

Bill: I just wanted to see how you're doing. How's your new place? You and Lourdes must be all settled in by now.

Luiz: Pretty much. But city life sure **takes some getting used to**.

Bill: In what way?

Luiz: Well, for one thing, not only do we have to deal with bumper-to-bumper traffic every day, but it's almost impossible to find on-the-street parking.

Bill: Yeah, that *is* a pain. Hey, what about your building? How's that worked out?

Luiz: Pretty well. It's safe and well-maintained. But, to be honest, it's been **a mixed blessing**.

Bill: What's the problem?

Luiz: Well, it's the neighbors on our floor. Whenever they hear someone get off the elevator, they look out their door to check who it is. I don't mean to sound unfriendly, but I wish they'd **mind their own business**.

Bill: Well, I'm sure they **mean well**. You should **look on the bright side**. It's good to be in a building where people **look out for each other**.

Luiz: That's true. We're very lucky. And I have to say, I've fallen in love with the neighborhood.

Bill: That's great!

Luiz: It's really **got a lot to offer**; we're never bored. Sometimes we go out for coffee and just people watch.

Bill: Well, all in all, it sounds like things are going well.

Luiz: They are. Hey, give my regards to Judy. And let me know if you're ever in town.

Bill: Will do!

E **UNDERSTAND IDIOMS AND EXPRESSIONS**   Write an expression from Spotlight for each definition.

1 choose to have an optimistic viewpoint ....

2 take care of other people ....

3 something that has both a good and bad side ....

4 not intrude in other people's lives ....

5 requires time to get comfortable with something ....

6 have good intentions ....

7 has many advantages ....

F **THINK AND EXPLAIN**   Answer the questions, supporting your answers with information from Spotlight.

1 What does Luiz like about the neighborhood he lives in, and what doesn't he like?

2 What does Luiz like about his building, and what doesn't he like?

SPEAKING   **PAIR WORK**   On a separate sheet of paper, list the pros and cons of living in a small town, a big city, and a suburb. Then compare opinions with a partner. Use expressions from Spotlight.

❝ What I don't like about living in the city is the bumper-to-bumper traffic. ❞

❝ Life in a small town is a mixed blessing. It's clean and quiet. But there's not much to do! ❞

LESSON 1

GOAL Politely ask someone not to do something

DIGITAL STRATEGIES

A ▶ 3:03 **WORD STUDY** **USING NEGATIVE PREFIXES TO FORM ANTONYMS**

Listen and repeat.

1 acceptable → **un**acceptable
2 considerate → **in**considerate
3 polite → **im**polite
4 proper → **im**proper
5 respectful → **dis**respectful
6 responsible → **ir**responsible

Negative prefixes
dis- ir-
im- un-
in-

B **WORD STUDY PRACTICE** Use a dictionary to find antonyms for these words. Then make a list of other adjectives with negative prefixes.

1 appropriate ....
2 courteous ....
3 excusable ....
4 imaginable ....
5 honest ....
6 pleasant ....
7 rational ....
8 mature ....

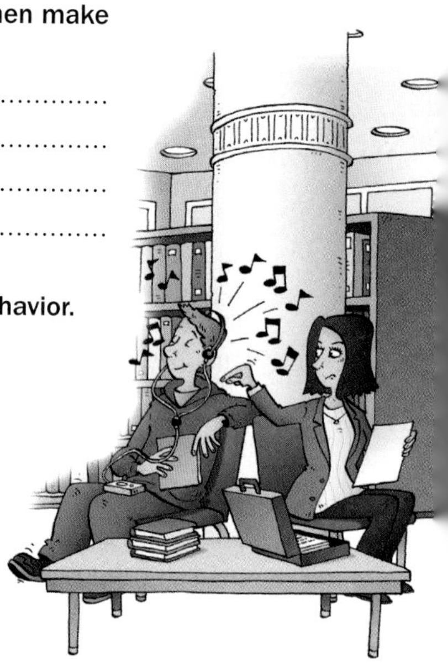

C **ACTIVATE WORD STUDY** Write sentences that describe inappropriate public behavior. Use adjectives from Exercises A and B.

Example: *It's inconsiderate to play loud music in the library.*

1 ....
2 ....
3 ....
4 ....
5 ....

D **PAIR WORK** Compare the examples you wrote in exercise C. Explain why you consider the behavior inappropriate.

DIGITAL INDUCTIVE ACTIVITY

E **GRAMMAR** **USING POSSESSIVE GERUNDS**

You can use a possessive gerund when you want to indicate the performer of the action.

I object to **their playing** loud music late at night.
Jack's talking during the movie was annoying.
Does **my daughter's playing** video games bother you?
What bothers me is **his not apologizing** for texting during class.

In informal spoken English, it is acceptable to use a name, a noun, or an object pronoun instead of a possessive, but only if the gerund phrase is the direct object in the sentence.

I object to **them playing** loud music late at night.

BUT Never use a name, noun, or an object pronoun if the gerund is the subject of the sentence. Use a possessive.

Their playing music late at night is a problem. NOT ~~Them playing~~ music late at night is a problem.

DIGITAL MORE EXERCISES

F **UNDERSTAND THE GRAMMAR** Write a check mark next to the sentences that are incorrect in speaking or writing. Correct them.

☐ 1 "Do you mind me eating lunch at my desk?"
☐ 2 "Your brother not saying hello to her was disrespectful."
☐ 3 "Kevin not agreeing to remove his shoes in my house was kind of impolite."
☐ 4 "Isn't Paula honking her car horn early in the morning inexcusable?"
☐ 5 "I don't like you answering your phone while we're eating dinner."

GRAMMAR PRACTICE   Combine the two statements, using a possessive gerund.

1 They allow smoking. I'm not in favor of it.

....*I'm not in favor of their allowing smoking.*..

2 He texted his friends during the concert. I didn't appreciate that.

....

3 They eat fast food in the car. Does your mother object to it?

....

4 She's talking on her cell phone. We don't mind it.

....

5 My brother didn't apologize. I'm really annoyed by it.

....

> **PRONUNCIATION BOOSTER**   p. 144
> Unstressed syllables: vowel reduction to /ə/

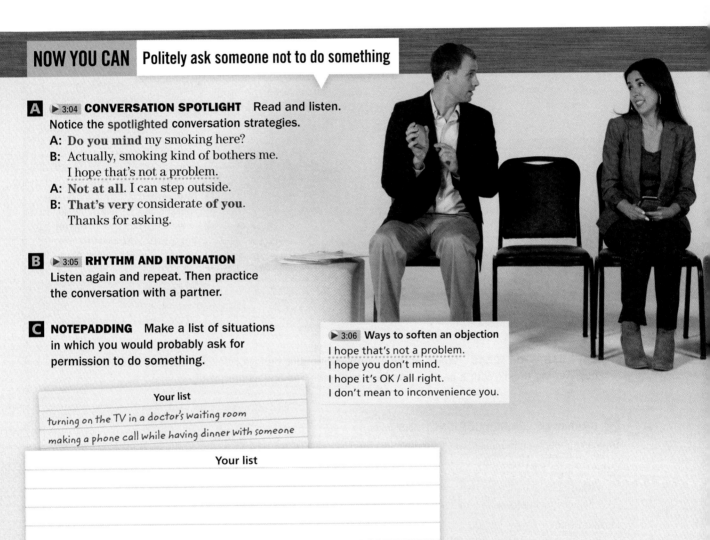

NOW YOU CAN   Politely ask someone not to do something

A ▶ 3:04 **CONVERSATION SPOTLIGHT**   Read and listen. Notice the spotlighted conversation strategies.

A: **Do you mind** my smoking here?
B: Actually, smoking kind of bothers me. I hope that's not a problem.
A: **Not at all**. I can step outside.
B: **That's very** considerate **of you**. Thanks for asking.

B ▶ 3:05 **RHYTHM AND INTONATION**
Listen again and repeat. Then practice the conversation with a partner.

C **NOTEPADDING**   Make a list of situations in which you would probably ask for permission to do something.

> ▶ 3:06 **Ways to soften an objection**
> I hope that's not a problem.
> I hope you don't mind.
> I hope it's OK / all right.
> I don't mean to inconvenience you.

Your list
turning on the TV in a doctor's waiting room
making a phone call while having dinner with someone

Your list

 D **CONVERSATION ACTIVATOR**   Create a conversation similar to the one in Exercise A, using a situation from your notepad. Start like this: *Do you mind my ... ?* Be sure to change roles and then partners.

DIGITAL VIDEO
DIGITAL SPEAKING BOOSTER

DON'T STOP!
• Explain why the behavior bothers you.
• Express understanding of your partner's point of view.
• Say as much as you can.

GOAL Complain about public conduct

A ▶3:07 **GRAMMAR SPOTLIGHT** Read the interview responses. Notice the spotlighted grammar.

What are some of your pet peeves?

cutting in line

"Well, it really bugs me when people cut in line at the theater! They should **either** arrive early enough for a good seat **or** wait in line patiently like everyone else does. Who do they think they are?"

Jean Seyedi
San Francisco, USA

littering on the street

"I'll tell you what really gets to me. I can **neither** tolerate **nor** understand people's littering in public places. Do they really expect others to clean up after them? That's just so inconsiderate. **Either** they should throw their garbage in a trash can **or** they should hold on to it till they find one."

Ken Becker
Philadelphia, USA

spitting on the sidewalk

"It really gets on my nerves when people spit on the street. **Not only** do I find it disgusting, **but** it's also unhygienic. It's important to think about public health and other people's feelings."

Nancy Shen
Shanghai, China

forgetting to turn off one's phone

"Here's a pet peeve of mine: I hate it when people forget to turn off their phones during a lecture or workshop. **Not only** is it distracting to the speaker, **but** it's also annoying to the audience. They should **either** have the courtesy to turn their phones off **or** simply leave them at home. It really ticks me off."

Paulo Acosta
Salvador, Brazil

B **EXPRESS YOUR IDEAS** Which of the examples of public behavior described in the interviews bug you the most? With a partner, compare your opinions and explain your reasons.

C **GRAMMAR** PAIRED CONJUNCTIONS
You can connect related ideas with paired conjunctions.

either ... or
  Either people should smoke outside **or** they shouldn't smoke at all.
  Phones should **either** be turned off **or** left at home.

neither ... nor
  I would allow **neither** spitting **nor** littering.
  Neither eating **nor** drinking is allowed in the lab.

not only ... but
Invert the subject and verb after Not only. Use a comma after the first clause.
  Not only is it dangerous to text while driving, **but** it may be illegal.
  Not only did they forget to turn off their phones, **but** they also talked during the concert.

Be careful!
When joining two subjects with either or neither, make sure the verb agrees with the subject nearer to the verb.
  Either the mayor or local businesspeople **need** to decide.
  Either local businesspeople or the mayor **needs** to decide.

GRAMMAR BOOSTER p. 133
· Conjunctions with so, too, neither, or not either
· So, too, neither, or not either: short responses

D **NOTICE THE GRAMMAR** Find an example of paired conjunctions in Spotlight on page 51.

E GRAMMAR PRACTICE   On a separate sheet of paper, combine the sentences, using the paired conjunction with <u>or</u>, <u>nor</u>, or <u>but (also)</u>.

1 People should speak up about what bothers them. They should just learn to live with other people's habits. (either)

2 It's rude when people talk on their phones in theaters. It's also rude when they talk on them on buses. (not only)

3 I hate the smell of cigarette smoke. I worry about the danger to my health. (not only)

4 My uncle isn't willing to give up smoking. My grandparents aren't willing to give up smoking. (neither)

NOW YOU CAN   Complain about public conduct

A NOTEPADDING   Make a list of some of your pet peeves in public places. Then write sentences with paired conjunctions to express your opinion. Use some of the adjectives with negative prefixes.

> In restaurants: *reading e-mail and texting during the meal*
> *Not only is it annoying, but it's also very impolite.*

In restaurants:
In stores:
On buses and trains:
On the street:
In offices:
In movie theaters:
Other:

Ideas
- cutting in line
- talking in theaters
- playing loud music
- honking a car horn
- not saying "Excuse me"

Adjectives with negative prefixes
disrespectful
immature
impolite
inconsiderate
inexcusable
irresponsible
unacceptable
unpleasant

B APPLY THE GRAMMAR   In a group, role play on-the-street interviews, with one student as the interviewer. Use your notepads and the Grammar Spotlight on page 54 as a guide.

> ❝What really ticks me off is ...❞

> ❝Here's what really gets on my nerves ...❞

> ❝I'll tell you what really gets to me ...❞

> ❝Do you want to know what bugs me?❞

C DISCUSSION ACTIVATOR   Discuss the questions. Say as much as you can.

1 In your opinion, how should people behave in public places? Do you think it's important to speak up when people behave inconsiderately in public?

2 Do *you* ever do things that annoy other people? Explain.

RECYCLE THIS LANGUAGE
- It takes getting used to.
- It's a mixed blessing.
- [They] should mind [their] own business.
- [They] mean well.
- Look on the bright side.

A READING WARM-UP Why do you think tourists might make ideal victims for criminals?

DIGITAL STRATEGIES **B** ▶ 3:08 **READING** Read the interview. Do you agree with Miller's advice?

DON'T LET URBAN CRIME SPOIL YOUR VISIT

Since the beginning of the century, there has been a steady increase in the number of foreign visitors to the great cities of the world. In this interview, travel writer Hanna Miller suggests ways for visitors to avoid becoming victims of urban crime.

You claim that tourists are particularly vulnerable to criminal activities. Why is that?

Miller: Well, for one thing, tourists are more likely than local people to be carrying large sums of money or valuables such as jewelry and electronics. They are also out of their comfort zone, being unfamiliar with local customs or places that should be avoided. Because they're enjoying themselves, tourists are more likely than locals to let their guard down, thinking they are safe when in fact they are not. And let's face it: tourists stand out. They look different and dress differently from the residents of the place they're visiting.

What kinds of crime do tourists need to be concerned about?

Miller: All kinds, including violent crime, unfortunately. Tourists, however, are primarily targeted for theft of the valuables they have on them and the information gained from passports, credit cards, and other forms of identification. Because out-of-town visitors tend to congregate at tourist attractions, it's easier for criminals to do their work. Not only does this provide the opportunity for a pickpocket to take someone's wallet unnoticed, but it also makes it easier for a purse-snatcher to quickly grab something and run. A mugger can follow a victim until he or she is alone at an ATM machine, for example, where the criminal can demand the victim's money and property.

So what precautions do you recommend?

Miller: Before you leave home, use the Internet to learn about your destination so you can avoid high-crime neighborhoods. The more you know, the better you can protect yourself. Photocopy your passport and make sure you have a list of all your credit card numbers. When you're packing, choose clothes that don't make you stand out as a tourist. By the way, the inside pocket of a jacket may seem like a good place for a wallet or passport, but it's a favorite target for pickpockets. You should either bring pants and jackets with zippered or buttoned pockets or consider buying a money belt. And leave unnecessary valuables at home!

And what extra precautions should tourists take in urban areas?

Miller: It goes without saying: Avoid streets that are not well-lit at night. And avoid going out alone, if you can. While there's usually safety in numbers, remember that tourist attractions also attract thieves. Stay aware of what's happening around you—as if you had eyes in the back of your head. On the street, avoid using a smart phone or tablet—or fumbling with a map or guidebook— if you don't need to. Be wary if a stranger asks for directions or starts up a conversation. He or she may be sizing you up as a potential victim. Be particularly careful in crowds at festivals or on buses or trains. Be suspicious of any sudden disruption. Thieves are known to intentionally create a distraction so you won't realize what they're actually doing. And a warning to women: Be careful if you wear a cross-body purse. It may be harder for a criminal to grab, but you could be injured if the purse snatcher is on a motorcycle.

Do people need to worry about leaving valuables in their hotel room?

Miller: Good point! Don't leave valuables unprotected in your room, where a burglar might break in and take them. Ask the front desk to keep them for you. Better safe than sorry! Finally, I should mention that, all in all, crime rates are going down worldwide, and the chances you will become a crime victim are low. So don't let worrying about crime interfere with your having a great time!

C CLASSIFY Look for the words pickpocket, purse snatcher, mugger, and burglar in the reading. Then choose the kind of criminal who committed each crime below.

1 "I was looking for souvenirs at the market when this kid grabs my bag!"
☐ a pickpocket   ☐ a purse snatcher   ☐ a mugger   ☐ a burglar

2 "I left my laptop in a dresser drawer under my dirty clothes, but when I got back to the hotel it was gone!"
☐ a pickpocket   ☐ a purse snatcher   ☐ a mugger   ☐ a burglar

3 "I was watching the parade when all of a sudden I realized someone had taken my passport!"
☐ a pickpocket   ☐ a purse snatcher   ☐ a mugger   ☐ a burglar

4 "We were walking on the beach, and three big guys surrounded us and demanded our wallets!"
☐ pickpockets   ☐ purse snatchers   ☐ muggers   ☐ burglars

D UNDERSTAND MEANING FROM CONTEXT Read each statement from the interview. Match each underlined expression with its meaning.

.... **1** They are also out of their comfort zone.

.... **2** Tourists are more likely than locals to let their guard down.

.... **3** Tourists stand out.

.... **4** … there's usually safety in numbers.

.... **5** He or she may be sizing you up.

a not be careful

b be more noticeable than others

c checking to see if you might be a good victim

d less risk by doing things with others

e doing what they're not accustomed to doing

E CRITICAL THINKING Discuss the questions. Support your ideas with examples.

1 What are some ways that tourists might let their guard down when traveling?

2 What should a visitor to your country do to not "look like a tourist?" What would *you* do to not look like one when you travel?

DIGITAL
EXTRA
CHALLENGE

NOW YOU CAN Suggest ways to avoid becoming a victim of urban crime

A NOTEPADDING With a partner, discuss ways to avoid becoming a crime victim in your own town or city for each situation on the notepad. Summarize your ideas.

B ROLE PLAY Imagine that you are a tourist visiting a new city, and your partner is a local. Tell your partner about what you've been doing during your visit. Your partner makes suggestions for how to avoid crime. Summarize your ideas on the notepad.

OPTIONAL WRITING Write a short guide for visitors to your city. Suggest how to stay safe and avoid becoming a crime victim.

while riding in a car
while using public transportation
while walking on the street
while staying in a hotel
while getting cash at an ATM machine
other

A ▶3:09 **LISTENING WARM-UP**   **VOCABULARY: COMMUNITY SERVICE ACTIVITIES**
Read and listen. Then listen again and repeat.

GET INVOLVED WITH YOUR COMMUNITY!

| Home | About | News | Community projects | Search 🔍 |

BEAUTIFY YOUR TOWN

Plant flowers or trees where there aren't any.

CLEAN UP LITTER
Pick up trash from parks, playgrounds, or the street.

RAISE MONEY

Mail letters, make phone calls, knock on doors, or set up a table to raise money for a charity or cause.

VOLUNTEER YOUR TIME
Work without pay in the fire department, a hospital, or a school.

DONATE BLOOD
Give the gift of life to someone who's very sick or has been in a serious accident.

B **VOCABULARY PRACTICE**   Would you ever consider doing any community service activities? With a partner, explain what you would, or would never, do.

> ❝ I would never consider **volunteering my time** to **clean up litter**. I think they should pay people to do that. ❞

Pete Frates is credited with starting the Ice Bucket Challenge.

C ▶3:10 **LISTEN TO SUMMARIZE**   Listen to the report about the Ice Bucket Challenge. What was it? Describe the idea in your own words.

D ▶3:11 **LISTEN FOR DETAILS**   Read the questions. Then listen again and answer them.

1 How much money did the Ice Bucket Challenge suggest donating if someone didn't take the challenge?

2 How much money was donated in just one month?

3 What percentage of the videos posted on Facebook actually led to donations?

☐ **1** It made people feel bad if they chose not to participate in the challenge.

☐ **2** There are more serious problems for which people could have donated money.

☐ **3** People should have paid more attention to the cause rather than on having fun.

☐ **4** The challenge didn't raise a lot of money for research.

☐ **5** Dumping ice water on your head could be dangerous.

☐ **6** Some celebrities took the challenge just to call attention to themselves.

F **EXPRESS AND SUPPORT AN OPINION**   Discuss the questions, using information from the report and your own ideas.

1 Do you think the Ice Bucket Challenge was a good idea? Do you agree with the critics or the supporters? Why?

2 Why do you think people on social media responded so strongly to the Ice Bucket Challenge?

NOW YOU CAN   Discuss the meaning of community

A **FRAME YOUR IDEAS**   With a partner, consider each situation and discuss what you might do. Based on your answers, how would you define the meaning of "community"?

1

There has been a terrible storm, and many homes have been destroyed. You're asked to let a family live with you until their home is fixed.

What would you say if they were ...

a. your relatives?

b. your neighbors?

c. your colleague's family?

d. complete strangers?

2

There has been a natural disaster with casualties, and someone needs a blood transfusion to survive. You have the same blood type and can donate your blood to save that person's life.

What would you do if the person were ...

a. a family member?

b. your neighbor?

c. your classmate?

d. a complete stranger?

❝My first responsibility is to my family. I can't imagine doing this for a total stranger.❞

❝Of course I'd help a stranger! It's the right thing to do.❞

3

Developers plan to destroy a historic tourist attraction so they can build a new office building. You're asked to donate your time to write letters and talk to your friends and colleagues to help save it.

What would you say if the tourist attraction were ...

a. in your neighborhood?

b. in another part of the city?

c. in another city in your country?

d. in another country?

DIGITAL
SPEAKING
BOOSTER
B **PAIR WORK**   Make a list of ideas for community projects in which you and your classmates could possibly participate. Share your list with the class and explain why you think your ideas would be worthwhile.

A WRITING SKILL Study the rules.

When writing to a friend or relative, it is acceptable to use an informal tone, casual language, and abbreviations. However, when writing to the head of a company, a boss, or someone you don't know, standard formal language should be used, and regular spelling and punctuation rules apply. Formal letters are usually typed, not handwritten. The following salutations and closings are appropriate for formal letters:

Formal salutations		Formal closings
If you know the name:	Dear Ms. Krum: Dear Mr. Paz: Dear Professor Lee: Dear Dr. Smith:	Sincerely, Respectfully, Best regards, Cordially,
If you don't know the name:	Dear Sir or Madam: To whom it may concern:	

Letters of Complaint

When writing a formal letter of complaint, first state the reason you are writing and describe the problem. Then inform whomever you are writing what you would like him or her to do about it, or what *you* plan to do. The language and tone in your message should be formal and polite.

WRITING MODEL

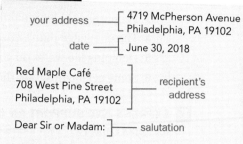

your address ── 4719 McPherson Avenue
Philadelphia, PA 19102

date ── June 30, 2018

Red Maple Café
708 West Pine Street ── recipient's address
Philadelphia, PA 19102

Dear Sir or Madam: ── salutation

I live a few blocks from your restaurant. For the past several months, I have noticed that in the evenings there is a lot of trash on the side of your building. Cats in the neighborhood turn over the garbage cans, and the trash goes everywhere. This is not only unpleasant to look at, but it is also a health hazard.

Could you please make sure that when the trash is put out, the garbage cans are closed? Your helping keep our neighborhood clean and beautiful would be greatly appreciated.

Respectfully, ── closing

Olivia Krum ── signature
Olivia Krum

B PRACTICE Write a salutation appropriate for a formal letter to each of these people.

1 a teacher at a university whose family name is Smith ....

2 a company manager whose name you don't know ....

3 a female company manager whose family name is Costa ....

4 a male bank manager whose family name is Takata ....

5 a physician who manages a clinic and whose family name is Grimond ....

DIGITAL WRITING PROCESS

C APPLY THE WRITING SKILL On a separate sheet of paper, write a letter of complaint about a problem in your city or town. State what you would like to see done to fix the problem. Remember to be polite and appropriately formal.

OPTIONAL WRITING Exchange letters with a partner. Write an appropriate response to your partner's letter, as if you were the person to whom it was addressed.

SELF-CHECK

☐ Did I use the proper salutation and closing?

☐ Are the tone and language in my letter appropriate for the intended reader?

☐ Did I use regular spelling and punctuation and avoid abbreviations?

A ▶ 3:13 Listen carefully to each story. Infer the type of criminal being described and complete the statements with the details of the crime.

1 A .... took his .... while he was riding on a ....

2 A .... stole .... from her while she was walking with a ....

3 He saw a .... running down the street with a girl's ....

4 A .... broke into her .... and took her husband's ....

B Respond to each statement or question in your own way.

1 "Your texting during the movie kind of bothers me."

You: ....

2 "Would you mind not smoking in here?"

You: ....

3 "What bugs you about living in your town?"

You: ....

4 "Who does things that really get to you?"

You: ....

C Make each sentence logical by attaching a negative prefix to the adjective. Use a dictionary if necessary.

1 Smoking on public buses and trains is really ~~excusable~~. *inexcusable*

2 I believe littering and spitting on the street are both ~~responsible~~.

3 People who play loud music without consideration for the people around them are exhibiting really ~~proper~~ behavior.

4 I think it's ~~appropriate~~ for people to text their friends during movies.

5 When a salesperson is rude, I find it not only ~~respectful~~ but also annoying.

6 I should warn you that the air pollution downtown is really ~~pleasant~~.

7 I think it's ~~honest~~ to sell souvenirs to tourists at higher prices than people usually pay.

8 It doesn't help when people are ~~courteous~~ to each other.

D Combine the sentences, using paired conjunctions.

1 Restaurants shouldn't allow smoking. Theaters shouldn't allow smoking. (neither … nor)

....

2 Smoking should be banned. It should be restricted. (either … or)

....

3 Littering doesn't offend me. Spitting doesn't offend me. (neither ... nor)

....

4 I think loud music is rude. I think loud people are rude. (Not only … but)

....

TEST-TAKING SKILLS BOOSTER p. 155

Web Project: Urban Communities
www.english.com/summit3e

Reference Charts

These are the pronunciation symbols used in **Summit 1**.

Vowels

Symbol	Key Word	Symbol	Key Word
i	beat, feed	ə	banana, among
ɪ	bit, did	ɚ	shirt, murder
eɪ	date, paid	aɪ	bite, cry, buy, eye
ɛ	bet, bed	aʊ	about, how
æ	bat, bad	ɔɪ	voice, boy
ɑ	box, odd, father	ɪr	beer
ɔ	bought, dog	ɛr	bare
oʊ	boat, road	ɑr	bar
ʊ	book, good	ɔr	door
u	boot, food, student	ʊr	tour
ʌ	but, mud, mother		

Consonants

Symbol	Key Word	Symbol	Key Word
p	pack, happy	z	zip, please, goes
b	back, rubber	ʃ	ship, machine, station, special, discussion
t	tie		
d	die		
k	came, key, quick	ʒ	measure, vision
g	game, guest	h	hot, who
tʃ	church, nature, watch	m	men, some
dʒ	judge, general, major	n	sun, know, pneumonia
f	fan, photograph	ŋ	sung, ringing
v	van	w	wet, white
θ	thing, breath	l	light, long
ð	then, breathe	r	right, wrong
s	sip, city, psychology	y	yes, use, music
		ţ	butter, bottle
		t̚	button

IRREGULAR VERBS

base form	simple past	past participle	base form	simple past	past participle
be	was / were	been	forget	forgot	forgotten
beat	beat	beaten	forgive	forgave	forgiven
become	became	become	freeze	froze	frozen
begin	began	begun	get	got	gotten
bend	bent	bent	give	gave	given
bet	bet	bet	go	went	gone
bite	bit	bitten	grow	grew	grown
bleed	bled	bled	hang	hung	hung
blow	blew	blown	have	had	had
break	broke	broken	hear	heard	heard
breed	bred	bred	hide	hid	hidden
bring	brought	brought	hit	hit	hit
build	built	built	hold	held	held
burn	burned / burnt	burned / burnt	hurt	hurt	hurt
burst	burst	burst	keep	kept	kept
buy	bought	bought	know	knew	known
catch	caught	caught	lay	laid	laid
choose	chose	chosen	lead	led	led
come	came	come	leap	leaped / leapt	leaped / leapt
cost	cost	cost	learn	learned / learnt	learned / learnt
creep	crept	crept	leave	left	left
cut	cut	cut	lend	lent	lent
deal	dealt	dealt	let	let	let
dig	dug	dug	lie	lay	lain
do	did	done	light	lit	lit
draw	drew	drawn	lose	lost	lost
dream	dreamed / dreamt	dreamed / dreamt	make	made	made
drink	drank	drunk	mean	meant	meant
drive	drove	driven	meet	met	met
eat	ate	eaten	mistake	mistook	mistaken
fall	fell	fallen	pay	paid	paid
feed	fed	fed	put	put	put
feel	felt	felt	quit	quit	quit
fight	fought	fought	read /rid/	read /rɛd/	read /rɛd/
find	found	found	ride	rode	ridden
fit	fit	fit	ring	rang	rung
fly	flew	flown	rise	rose	risen
forbid	forbade	forbidden	run	ran	run

base form	simple past	past participle	base form	simple past	past participle
say	said	said	spring	sprang / sprung	sprung
see	saw	seen	stand	stood	stood
sell	sold	sold	steal	stole	stolen
send	sent	sent	stick	stuck	stuck
set	set	set	sting	stung	stung
shake	shook	shaken	stink	stank / stunk	stunk
shed	shed	shed	strike	struck	struck / stricken
shine	shone	shone	string	strung	strung
shoot	shot	shot	swear	swore	sworn
show	showed	shown	sweep	swept	swept
shrink	shrank	shrunk	swim	swam	swum
shut	shut	shut	swing	swung	swung
sing	sang	sung	take	took	taken
sink	sank	sunk	teach	taught	taught
sit	sat	sat	tear	tore	torn
sleep	slept	slept	tell	told	told
slide	slid	slid	think	thought	thought
smell	smelled / smelt	smelled / smelt	throw	threw	thrown
speak	spoke	spoken	understand	understood	understood
speed	sped / speeded	sped / speeded	upset	upset	upset
spell	spelled / spelt	spelled / spelt	wake	woke / waked	woken / waked
spend	spent	spent	wear	wore	worn
spill	spilled / spilt	spilled / spilt	weave	wove	woven
spin	spun	spun	weep	wept	wept
spit	spit / spat	spit / spat	win	won	won
spoil	spoiled / spoilt	spoiled / spoilt	wind	wound	wound
spread	spread	spread	write	wrote	written

STATIVE VERBS

amaze	desire	hear	need	seem
appear*	dislike	imagine	owe	smell*
appreciate	doubt	include*	own	sound
astonish	envy	know	please	suppose
be*	equal	like	possess	surprise
believe	exist	look like	prefer	taste*
belong	fear	look*	realize	think*
care	feel*	love	recognize	understand
consist of	forget	matter	remember*	want*
contain	hate	mean	resemble	weigh*
cost	have*	mind	see*	

*These verbs also have action meanings. Example: *I see a tree.* (non-action) *I'm seeing her tomorrow.* (action)

VERBS FOLLOWED BY A GERUND

acknowledge	consider	endure	imagine	prevent	resent
admit	delay	enjoy	justify	prohibit	resist
advise	deny	escape	keep	propose	risk
appreciate	detest	explain	mention	quit	suggest
avoid	discontinue	feel like	mind	recall	support
can't help	discuss	finish	miss	recommend	tolerate
celebrate	dislike	forgive	postpone	report	understand
complete	don't mind	give up	practice		

EXPRESSIONS THAT CAN BE FOLLOWED BY A GERUND

be excited about	be opposed to	believe in	blame [someone or something] for
be worried about	be used to	participate in	forgive [someone or something] for
be responsible for	complain about	succeed in	thank [someone or something] for
be interested in	dream about / of	take advantage of	keep [someone or something] from
be accused of	talk about / of	take care of	prevent [someone or something] from
be capable of	think about / of	insist on	stop [someone or something] from
be tired of	apologize for	look forward to	
be accustomed to	make an excuse for		
be committed to	have a reason for		

VERBS FOLLOWED DIRECTLY BY AN INFINITIVE

afford	choose	grow	mean	pretend	threaten
agree	claim	hesitate	need	promise	volunteer
appear	consent	hope	neglect	refuse	wait
arrange	decide	hurry	offer	request	want
ask	demand	intend	pay	seem	wish
attempt	deserve	learn	plan	struggle	would like
can't wait	expect	manage	prepare	swear	yearn
care	fail				

VERBS FOLLOWED BY AN OBJECT BEFORE AN INFINITIVE*

advise	choose*	force	need*	remind	urge
allow	convince	get*	order	request	want*
ask*	enable	help*	pay	require	warn
beg	encourage	hire	permit	teach	wish*
cause	expect*	instruct	persuade	tell	would like*
challenge	forbid	invite	promise*		

*In the active voice, these verbs can be followed by the infinitive without an object (example: *want to speak* or *want someone to speak*).

ADJECTIVES FOLLOWED BY AN INFINITIVE*

afraid	content	disturbed	glad	proud	sorry
alarmed	curious	eager	happy	ready	surprised
amazed	delighted	easy	hesitant	relieved	touched
angry	depressed	embarrassed	likely	reluctant	upset
anxious	determined	encouraged	lucky	sad	willing
ashamed	disappointed	excited	pleased	shocked	
certain	distressed	fortunate	prepared		

*Example: *I'm willing **to accept** that.*

VERBS THAT CAN BE FOLLOWED BY A GERUND OR AN INFINITIVE

with a change in meaning

forget (+ gerund)	=	forget something that happened
(+ infinitive)	=	forget something that needs to be done
regret (+ gerund)	=	regret a past action
(+ infinitive)	=	regret having to inform someone about an action
remember (+ gerund)	=	remember something that happened
(+ infinitive)	=	remember something that needs to be done
stop (+ gerund)	=	stop a continuous action
(+ infinitive)	=	stop in order to do something

without a change in meaning

begin	love
can't stand	prefer
continue	start
hate	try
like	

PARTICIPIAL ADJECTIVES

alarming	–	alarmed	disturbing	–	disturbed
amazing	–	amazed	embarrassing	–	embarrassed
amusing	–	amused	entertaining	–	entertained
annoying	–	annoyed	exciting	–	excited
astonishing	–	astonished	exhausting	–	exhausted
boring	–	bored	fascinating	–	fascinated
comforting	–	comforted	frightening	–	frightened
confusing	–	confused	horrifying	–	horrified
depressing	–	depressed	inspiring	–	inspired
disappointing	–	disappointed	interesting	–	interested
disgusting	–	disgusted	irritating	–	irritated
distressing	–	distressed	moving	–	moved

paralyzing	–	paralyzed
pleasing	–	pleased
relaxing	–	relaxed
satisfying	–	satisfied
shocking	–	shocked
soothing	–	soothed
startling	–	startled
stimulating	–	stimulated
surprising	–	surprised
terrifying	–	terrified
tiring	–	tired
touching	–	touched

Grammar Booster

The Grammar Booster is optional. It offers more information and extra practice, as well as Grammar for Writing. Sometimes it further explains or expands the unit grammar and points out common errors. In other cases, it reviews and practices previously learned grammar that would be helpful when learning new grammar concepts. If you use the Grammar Booster, you will find extra exercises in the Workbook in a separate section labeled Grammar Booster. The Grammar Booster content is not tested on any *Summit* tests.

UNIT 1

Infinitives: review, expansion, and common errors

Statements

Using an infinitive as the subject of a sentence sounds extremely formal in speaking. There are two ways to express the same idea: (1) Make the infinitive a subject complement, or (2) use an impersonal <u>it</u>.

To be a mother is my greatest wish. →
1 My greatest wish is **to be** a mother.
2 **It's** my greatest wish **to be** a mother.

When making a statement with an impersonal <u>It</u> and an infinitive about a specific person or people, use a phrase with <u>for</u> + a noun or a pronoun to name that person or people.

It isn't hard **for me** to learn new languages.
It usually takes time **for new students** to get to know each other.
It's too late **for Ella and Paul** to go out for dinner now.

With causative <u>get</u>

Use an infinitive, not a base form, with causative <u>get</u>.

We **got** everyone **to fill out** the survey.
The teacher **got** me **to compare** my personality with my mother's personality.

In indirect speech

Use an infinitive to replace an imperative in indirect speech.

The manager said, "Be at the meeting at 2:15 sharp." → The manager said **to be** at the meeting at 2:15 sharp.
She told us, "Don't call before dinner." → She told us **not to call** before dinner.

> **Be careful!** You can't use an adjective of feeling or emotion in statements with <u>It's</u> + adjective and infinitive. You have to use an actual subject.
> **My sister** is happy to graduate.
> NOT ~~It's~~ happy to graduate.

> **Some adjectives of feeling or emotion:**
> | | | | |
> |---|---|---|---|
> | afraid | ashamed | excited | sad |
> | amazed | depressed | glad | shocked |
> | angry | disappointed | happy | sorry |
> | anxious | embarrassed | pleased | upset |

A On a separate sheet of paper, rewrite each sentence, changing the subject infinitive to a subject complement.

1 To be successful is every new graduate's wish.
2 To cook dinner is my chore for the evening.
3 To win the game is every player's dream.
4 To rescue hikers lost in the woods is the responsibility of the park police.
5 To win the election is every candidate's task.

B Rewrite each sentence, beginning with an impersonal <u>it</u>.

1 To be disciplined about an exercise program is difficult for an easygoing person.
2 To get to work on time is a good idea.
3 To be outgoing in new situations is helpful.
4 To act friendly is always worthwhile.
5 To be too talkative can sometimes be a problem.
6 To pass the examination is not the easiest thing in the world.
7 To live in an English-speaking country might be an exciting experience.
8 To know when to use an infinitive and when to use a gerund is pretty confusing.

C Insert a phrase with <u>for</u> in each of the following sentences.

1 It's hard *for new drivers* to drive in a lot of traffic.
2 It's important to remember that some difficult things are just a part of life.
3 It's smart to realize that it's better to be safe than sorry.
4 It's too late to make the early show.
5 It's essential to use insect repellent when you camp in the woods.
6 It's good to avoid being too outgoing when you're starting a new job.

D On a separate sheet of paper, rewrite each statement in indirect speech.

1 Celine said, "Don't be late for the meeting."

2 Last night they told me, "Always take care when you go out in the evening."

3 My sister said, "Don't call me before 7:00 A.M."

4 The tour guide told them, "Just roll with the punches."

✏ Grammar for Writing: parallelism with gerunds and infinitives

A common error in formal written English is mixing gerunds and infinitives when listing items in a series. A list of items should be either all gerunds or all infinitives.

When I take time off from work, I prefer **relaxing** at home, **spending** time with my family, and **getting** things done around the house.

NOT I prefer relaxing at home, spending time with my family, and to get things done around the house.

I can't stand **getting up** late and **missing** the bus. NOT I can't stand getting up late and to miss the bus.

In a series, either use <u>to</u> with all the infinitives or use it only with the first one.

When I take time off from work, I prefer **to relax** at home, **spend** time with my family, and **get** things done around the house. NOT When I take time off from work, I prefer to relax at home, spend time with my family, and to get things done around the house.

E On a separate sheet of paper, correct the errors in parallelism in the following sentences.

1 After she arrived in London, she began to write long letters home and calling her parents at all hours of the night.

2 There are two things I really can't stand doing: speaking in front of large audiences and chat with people I don't know at parties.

3 Right before midnight, everyone began to sing, dance, and to welcome in the new year.

4 There's no question I prefer using all my vacation time and take a long vacation.

F Complete the following sentences, using appropriate gerund or infinitive forms. Refer to pages 122–124 in the Reference Charts if necessary.

1 I would suggest .... out the form immediately and .... a copy for your records.
   fill .... make

2 Did you remember .... off the stove, ... the windows, and .... the door before you left?
   turn .... close .... lock

3 It's obvious from her e-mails that she really loves .... the culture, ... new people, and just .... there.
   experience .... meet .... be

4 They prohibit .... photographs or .... a recorder.
   take .... use

5 I really wouldn't mind .... them out to dinner or .... them around if you'd like me to.
   take .... show

6 He promised .... the report home, ... it carefully, and .... to any questions by the next day.
   take .... read .... respond

---

UNIT 2

Finished and unfinished actions: summary

Finished actions

Use the simple past tense or the past of <u>be</u> for an action finished at a specified time in the past.

They **watched** some movies yesterday.

Use the present perfect for an action finished at an unspecified time in the past.

They**'ve watched** that movie three times.

Use the past perfect for an action that was finished before another action in the past.

When I arrived, they **had** already **watched** the movie.

Note: Although the continuous aspect is used for actions in progress, the present perfect continuous is sometimes used for very recently completed actions, especially to emphasize duration.

They**'ve been watching** movies all afternoon, but they're done now.

Unfinished actions

Use the past continuous for unfinished actions that continued for a period of time or during a specific time in the past.

I **was relaxing** at home all morning.

At noon, I **was watching** a movie.

Use the present perfect OR the present perfect continuous for unfinished actions that began in the past and may continue into the future. Use the present perfect continuous to further emphasize that the action is continuous.

She**'s listened** to R&B for years. [And she may continue.]

OR She**'s been listening** to R&B for years. [And she may continue.]

A Complete the article, using the simple past tense, the past of <u>be</u>, or the present perfect.

World Music is not really a true genre of music—it is a combination of musical genres from around the world. More recently recording companies .... the term to describe the music of artists who
1 use

they felt could appeal to new audiences across cultures. The concept of World Music .... first
2 be

created after U.S. singer / songwriter Paul Simon .... his hugely successful *Graceland* album
3 record

in 1986. At that time, he .... South Africa's male choir Ladysmith Black Mambazo and rock
4 invite

group Savuka to accompany him on the recording. Both groups later .... with him around
5 tour

the world. This exciting collaboration immediately .... to European and North American
6 appeal

audiences, who were attracted to this different sound.

Since that time, as more artists .... to reach new audiences, there .... an
7 try   8 be

increased amount of "crossover"—that is, musicians influencing each other across cultures. Enthusiasm for

music from other cultures .... steadily. Artists such as Angélique Kidjo and Carlos Vives, who
9 rise

were well-known within specific regions such as Africa or Latin America, ... international
10 become

stars, and mainstream music .... many of the features of these artists.
11 incorporate

B Read each statement. Then decide which description is closer in meaning.

1 By the time I heard about it, the concert had sold out.

  a First I heard about the concert. Then it sold out.

  b First the concert sold out. Then I heard about it.

2 After he'd won the award, he got a big recording contract.

  a First he got the recording contract. Then he won the award.

  b First he won the award. Then he got the recording contract.

3 We wanted to go to his performance because we'd heard his new album.

  a First we heard his album. Then we wanted to go to his performance.

  b First we wanted to go to his performance. Then we heard his album.

4 He'd played at a lot of different halls before he performed at Carnegie Hall.

  a First he performed at Carnegie Hall. Then he played at a lot of different halls.

  b First he played at a lot of different halls. Then he performed at Carnegie Hall.

Noun clauses: review and expansion

Remember: A noun clause functions as a noun and is often introduced with <u>that</u>. When a noun clause is a direct object, use of <u>that</u> is optional.

> I didn't realize **(that) art therapy could be so helpful**.

Introduce a noun clause with <u>if</u> or <u>whether</u> when it is an embedded <u>yes</u> / <u>no</u> question. Use a question word when it is an embedded information question.

> (Does she come from the U.S.?) Do you know **if she comes from the U.S.**?
> (When does the concert begin?) I'm not sure **when the concert begins**.

A noun clause can also function as the subject of a sentence. A noun clause introduced with a question word can also function as a subject complement.

> **What he said** was very interesting. (subject)
> **That she's a therapist** surprises me. (subject)
> Teaching children is **what I love**. (subject complement)

Be careful! Don't use question word order in noun clauses that are embedded questions.

> I don't know **where the band is performing**.
>   NOT I don't know ~~where is the band~~ performing.
> Does he understand **what the lyrics mean**?
>   NOT Does he understand ~~what do the lyrics~~ mean?

Use a period with an embedded question within a statement. Use a question mark with an embedded question within a question.

> **I don't know** who is singing**.**
> **Do you know** who is singing**?**

C Complete each noun clause with <u>that</u>, <u>if</u> (or <u>whether</u>), or a question word. (Some have more than one possible answer.)

1 She thinks .... classical music is boring.

2 Catching up with friends on social media is .... I spend Saturday mornings.

3 I don't remember .... bands we saw in concert last year.

4 .... I like most is electronic pop.

5 Did anyone tell you .... I'm showing my paintings at the Henderson gallery?

6 Robert asked me .... I had bought tickets for the ballet yet.

7 I can't imagine .... life would be like without the arts.

8 I don't really know .... to cook very well.

9 New York is .... the Empire State Building is located.

10 I wonder .... the concert begins.

D Complete each statement, using a noun clause based on the question in parentheses.

1 (Where did Mozart live?) I don't know ....

2 (What type of music does our teacher like?) I have no idea ....

3 (When did the Black Eyed Peas recently perform in Chicago?) She asked me ....

4 (Are ballet tickets really expensive?) I don't know ....

5 (How long is the musical Annie?) I'm not sure ....

6 (Will the movie end before 6:00?) He's asking ....

✎ Grammar for Writing: noun clauses as adjective and noun complements

As adjective complements

To more formally make a point, use <u>It</u> + <u>be</u> or another linking verb + an adjective with a noun clause beginning with <u>that</u>. <u>That</u> is optional.

> **It is clear (that)** Hensley has done a lot of research.
> **It seems obvious (that)** the band needs a new lead singer.
> **It was surprising (that)** they never performed together again.

As noun complements

To more formally focus on an issue or topic, complete the meaning of a noun phrase with a noun clause. <u>That</u> is necessary.

> The fact **that her songs were extremely popular** made her very wealthy.
> The belief **that vaccines might be harmful** led some people to refuse them.

Some adjectives used in expressions with <u>It</u> + <u>be</u> or another linking verb:

It	is was will be could be seems	obvious important essential unacceptable surprising interesting	(that)

Some noun phrases used to introduce noun clauses:

The announcement that	The idea that
The argument that	The news that
The belief that	The possibility that
The chance that	The proposal that
The claim that	The recommendation that
The demand that	The report that
The fact that	The suggestion that

E On a separate sheet of paper, rewrite each sentence, using <u>It</u> + <u>be</u> (or a linking verb) + an adjective and a noun clause as an adjective complement.

1 That developing countries address the problems caused by global warming is extremely important.

2 That the president plans on resigning appears obvious to everyone.

3 That not providing disaster relief will only worsen the situation seems quite clear.

4 That a cure for cancer will be discovered in the next twenty years is certainly possible.

5 That the governments of Argentina and Chile will reach an agreement looks very likely.

6 That Max Bianchi won't be participating in the Olympics next year is not important.

F Read each quote from a radio news program. Then, on a separate sheet of paper, complete each statement, using the noun clause as a noun complement.

Example: "Volkswagen announced **that they would unveil a new car design early next year**. This is causing a lot of excitement in the auto industry." [The announcement …]

> The announcement that Volkswagen would unveil a new car design
> early next year is causing a lot of excitement in the auto industry.

1 "The Health Ministry announced **that they will begin vaccinating all infants for measles.** This was greeted with criticism from the opposition party." [The announcement …]

2 "The president said it was possible **that he would resign by the end of this year**. This has taken everyone by surprise, including the news media." [The possibility …]

3 "The London Sun reports **that Dr. Regina Blair of the Glasgow Medical Center has discovered a new protein.** This is attracting much interest in the world of science." [The report …]

4 "The Auckland Times claimed **that a ninety-five-year-old New Zealand man had broken the world record for growing the longest beard**. This has triggered similar claims across three continents." [The claim …]

UNIT 3

The past unreal conditional: inverted form

The conditional clause of past unreal conditional sentences can be stated without <u>if</u> by simply inverting <u>had</u> and the subject of the clause. Clauses using inverted word order are more formal than those using usual (non-inverted) word order.

> **Be careful!** Don't contract <u>not</u> with <u>had</u> in inverted negative clauses.
>
> Had they not been there, they wouldn't have known the truth. NOT ~~Hadn't~~ they been there, they wouldn't have known the truth.

Usual word order		Inverted word order
If I had known it would take up so much room, I wouldn't have bought it.	→	**Had I known** it would take up so much room, I wouldn't have bought it.
I might have gotten another brand **if I had realized** it would be so hard to operate.	→	I might have gotten another brand **had I realized** it would be so hard to operate.
If we hadn't been so busy, we could have shopped around.	→	**Had we not been** so busy, we could have shopped around.
If she had told me this thing wouldn't operate without batteries, I would never have considered getting it.	→	**Had she told** me this thing wouldn't operate without batteries, I would never have considered getting it.

A On a separate sheet of paper, rewrite the following past unreal conditional sentences, using the inverted form.

1 They would have lent her their car if she had asked.

2 If I hadn't spent so much money on my vacation, I would have considered buying a stationary bicycle.

3 If the Carsons hadn't moved into such a small apartment, they would have bought a treadmill.

4 Could you have gotten the car if they hadn't raised the price?

B On a separate sheet of paper, complete the statements of buyer's remorse, using the inverted form and the Vocabulary from page 28.

1 … I would never have gotten that espresso maker.

2 … we never would have bought such a large sofa.

3 … I could have gotten an entertainment center with fewer pieces.

4 … we probably would have bought a more economical car.

5 … I would have gotten a DVR with simpler directions.

The future continuous

Use the future continuous for actions that will be in progress at a specific time or over a period of time in the future. To form the future continuous, use <u>will</u> + <u>be</u> + a present participle OR <u>be going to</u> + <u>be</u> + a present participle.

At this time next week, I { **'ll be lying** / **'m going to be lying** } on a beach in Hawaii. [specific time]

I { **'ll be studying** / **'m going to be studying** } English in the United States for about two years. [period of time]

Sometimes sentences in the simple future and the future continuous have almost the same meaning. Choose the future continuous to emphasize a continuous or uninterrupted activity.

Next year, I'**ll study** English in the United States.

Next year, I'**ll be studying** English in the United States.

Questions and short answers

Will you **be working** at home? Yes, I **will**. / No, I **won't**.

Are you **going to be working** at home? Yes, I **am**. / No, I'**m not**.

Use the future continuous and a time clause with <u>while</u> or <u>when</u> to describe a continuous activity that will occur at the same time as another activity. Do not use a future form in the time clause.

I'**ll be looking** for a job while my wife **continues** her studies.

  NOT I'll be looking for a job while my wife ~~will be continuing~~ her studies.

When the teacher **is speaking**, we'**ll be listening** carefully.

  NOT When the teacher ~~will be speaking~~, we'll be listening carefully.

> **Remember:** Don't use a continuous form with a stative verb. Stative verbs are "non-action" verbs such as <u>be</u>, <u>have</u>, <u>know</u>, <u>remember</u>, <u>like</u>, <u>seem</u>, <u>appreciate</u>, etc.
>
> Do not use the continuous with stative verbs.
>   DON'T SAY By next month, ~~I'll be having~~ a new car.
>
> For a complete list of stative verbs, see page 123 in the Reference Charts.

C On a separate sheet of paper, correct the errors in the following sentences.

1 She'll be staying at the Newton Hotel when she's going to be attending the meeting.

2 We won't be spending much time sightseeing while we'll be visiting London.

3 When he's going to stay in town, he's going to be meeting with some friends.

4 She'll be correcting homework while the students will take the test.

5 While Michelle will be serving dessert, Randy will already be washing the dishes.

6 Won't they be going to sleep in New York when you'll be getting up in Taipei?

D Complete the following sentences, using the future continuous with <u>will</u> when possible. If the future continuous is not possible, use the simple future with <u>will</u>.

1 After I've completed my studies, I .... for a job.

                                    look

2 She .... historic sites while she's in Turkey.

            photograph

3 In a few years, they .... all the problems they had.

                not / remember

4 .... he .... very long between flights?

                           wait

5 I'm sure she .... when you call tonight.

              not / sleep

The future perfect continuous

Use the future perfect continuous to emphasize the continuous quality of an action that began before a specific time in the future. To form the future perfect continuous, use <u>will</u> (or <u>won't</u>) + <u>have been</u> and a present participle.

By next year, I'**ll have been studying** English for five years. [Describes an action that began before "next year" and may still continue.]

Combine a statement using the future perfect continuous with a time clause to show the relationship between two future actions. Use the simple present tense in the time clause.

By the time I arrive in New York, I'**ll have been sitting** in a plane for over ten hours.
NOT By the time I'll arrive in New York, I'll have been sitting in a plane for over ten hours.

E Complete the postcard, using the future continuous or the future perfect continuous.

Dear Ida,

Venice was great, but finally on to Paris! By tomorrow afternoon, I .... down

the Champs Elysées and .... in the beautiful sights of that great city.
2 take

In the evening, I .... an opera by Bizet in the city where he was born.
3 enjoy

Just think, by Saturday, I .... delicious French food for a whole week!
4 eat

Plus, I .... my French with real native speakers. Then, after Paris, it's off to
5 practice

the Riviera, where I .... around on the beaches of Nice and Saint-Tropez
6 lounge

for a week. By that time, I .... for three weeks, and it will almost be time
7 travel

to come home—a long trip for a homebody like me!

See you soon!

Pavel

1 stroll

UNIT 4

Quantifiers: <u>a few</u> and <u>few</u>, <u>a little</u> and <u>little</u>

Use <u>a few</u> with plural count nouns and <u>a little</u> with non-count nouns to mean "some."
Use <u>few</u> with plural count nouns and <u>little</u> with non-count nouns to mean "not many" or "not much."

A few / few
 A few companies are allowing their employees to dress casually on Fridays. [= some companies]
 Few companies are allowing their employees to dress casually on Fridays. [= not many companies]

A little / little
 Employees are showing **a little interest** in this new dress code. [= some interest]
 Employees are showing **little interest** in this new dress code. [= not much interest]

Quantifiers used without referents
Quantifiers can be used without the noun they describe, as long as the context has been made clear earlier.
 Most people don't think we'll find life on other planets in our lifetime, but **a few** do.
 Several workers in our office think people should dress down every day, but **most** don't.

A Change the underlined quantifiers to <u>a few</u>, <u>few</u>, <u>a little</u>, or <u>little</u>.

1 Would you like to listen to <u>some</u> music? *a little*

2 We actually eat <u>almost no</u> meat.

3 There were <u>several</u> new students in my class today.

4 I've seen <u>hardly any</u> movies in the last month.

5 I enjoy visiting Ames, but there's <u>not much</u> to do there.

6 If you look in the fridge, there should be <u>some</u> eggs.

Quantifiers: using of for specific reference

Use of when a noun is preceded by a possessive adjective, a possessive noun, a demonstrative adjective, or the article the.

More general	More specific
any friends	**any of** her friends
some students	**some of** his students
one cat	**one of** my cats
all employees	**all of** our employees
most co-workers	**most of** Jack's co-workers
several companies	**several of** these companies
many books	**many of** those books
a few choices	**a few of** the choices
a little cake	**a little of** the cake

> **possessive adjectives** = my, her, their, etc.
> **possessive nouns** = John's, the doctor's
> **demonstrative adjectives** = this, that, these, those

Using of after all or both is optional, with no change in meaning.

all of our employees	OR	**all** our employees	NOT	**all** ~~of~~ employees
both of those choices	OR	**both** those choices	NOT	**both** ~~of~~ choices

One and each are used with singular nouns only. But one of and each of are used with plural nouns only. However, the meaning of both expressions is still singular.

One student	—	**One of** the students
Each class	—	**Each of** the classes

Some quantifiers must include of when they modify a noun or noun phrase.

a lot of	a majority of	a couple of	a bit of
lots of	plenty of	a number of	a great deal of

> **Be careful!** In the superlative, do not use of after most.
> DON'T SAY Tokyo is the city with the most ~~of~~ people in Japan.
>
> Of must be included when using an object pronoun.
> **both of** them NOT ~~both them~~

B Only one of each pair of sentences is correct. Check the correct sentence and correct the mistake in the other one.

1 a ✓ She went with several of her classmates.

   b ☐ Several ~~of~~ classmates went out for coffee.

2 a ☐ Most of companies in the world are fairly formal.

   b ☐ Most of the companies in the United States have dress-down days.

3 a ☐ All of hot appetizers were delicious.

   b ☐ Everyone tried all of the cold appetizers.

4 a ☐ A lot of my friends have traveled to exotic places.

   b ☐ There are a lot places I'd like to see.

5 a ☐ I read a few of Steinbeck's novels last year.

   b ☐ A few of novels by Steinbeck take place in Mexico.

6 a ☐ Several managers were interviewed, and many them liked the new policy.

   b ☐ Many of the employees we spoke with liked the new policy.

Grammar for Writing: subject-verb agreement of quantifiers followed by of

In quantifiers with of, the verb must agree with the noun that comes after of.

Some of **the movie is** in English.	—	Some of **the movies are** in English.
A lot of **the music was** jazz.	—	A lot of **the musicians were** young.

In formal written English, none of is traditionally followed by a singular verb. However, in spoken English it is almost always used with a plural verb. The plural verb is acceptable and correct.

Formal: **None of** the students **was** late for class.

Informal: **None of** the students **were** late for class.

> **Be careful!** The quantifiers one of, each of, and every one of are always followed by a plural noun, but they always take a singular verb.
> **One of** the students **likes** rap music.

C Choose the verb that agrees with each subject.

1 Every one of these choices (sound / sounds) terrific!

2 One of the teachers (was / were) going to stay after class.

3 A lot of the problem (is / are) that no one wants to work so hard.

4 Each of the employees (want / wants) to work overtime.

5 Half of the city (was / were) flooded in the storm.

6 None of the players (is coming / are coming) to the game.

7 Only 8 percent of their workers prefer shorter work weeks, while at least 90 percent (don't / doesn't).

UNIT 5

Conjunctions with so, too, neither, or not either

Use and so or and ... too to join affirmative statements that are similar.

Spitting on the street is offensive, **and so** is littering. OR ..., **and** littering is, **too**.

Playing loud music bothers me, **and so** does smoking. OR ..., **and** smoking does, **too**.

Use and neither or and ... not either to join negative statements that are similar.

Playing loud music isn't polite, **and neither** is smoking. OR ... **and** smoking is**n't either**.

Spitting on the street doesn't bother me, **and neither** does littering. OR ... **and** littering does**n't either**.

If the first clause uses the verb be, an auxiliary verb, or a modal, use the same structure in the second clause.

Tokyo **is** a huge city, and so **is** São Paulo.

New York **doesn't** have a lot of industry, and neither **does** London.

Mexico City **has** grown a lot, and so **has** Los Angeles.

Nancy **can't** tolerate loud music, and neither **can** Tom.

I **haven't** been to Tokyo, and neither **have** you.

If the first clause is an affirmative statement in the simple present or simple past tense, use do, does, or did in the second clause.

John **thinks** graffiti is a big problem, and so **does** Helen.

My wife **enjoyed** visiting Paris, and so **did** I.

> **Notice the subject-verb order.**
> ... and so **is littering**.
> ... and **littering is**, too.
>
> ... and neither **does littering**.
> ... and **littering doesn't** either.

> **Be careful!**
> Use a negative verb, auxiliary verb, or modal with either and an affirmative with neither.
> ... and littering **doesn't either**.
> NOT ... and littering ~~does either~~.
> ... and **neither does** littering.
> NOT ... and ~~neither doesn't~~ littering.
>
> With so and neither, the verb (or auxiliary verb or modal) goes before the subject.
> Tokyo is a huge city, and so **is São Paulo**.
> NOT ... and so ~~São Paulo is~~.
> Nancy can't stand loud music, and neither **can Tom**.
> NOT ... neither ~~Tom can~~.

A Find and underline the nine errors. On a separate sheet of paper, write each sentence correctly.

New York is one of the most famous cities in the world, and so does London. While these two cities differ in many ways, they also share a number of characteristics. Here's a quick comparison:

- If you're looking for peace and quiet, New York is not the place to be, and neither London is. They are both exciting and noisy places. If you're not used to it, New York's traffic can be deafening at times, and so does London's.

- The best way to get around in both cities is the subway (or the Tube in London). New York's subway system is quite old and elaborate, and is London's, too.

- If you're looking for first-rate entertainment, New York is filled with theaters, and so London does.

- Hungry? London's restaurants feature exciting dishes from around the world, and New York's are, too.

- Both cities offer a huge choice of museums to visit. The museums in New York can't possibly be seen in a day, and either London's can't.

- New York offers some of the world's most famous tourist sites—for example, the Statue of Liberty and the Empire State Building—and so is London, with Buckingham Palace and the Millennium Wheel.

It's clear that New York shouldn't be missed, and neither London shouldn't!

B On a separate sheet of paper, rewrite each statement, using the word in parentheses. Make any necessary changes in verbs or possessive adjectives.

Example: Both Quito and Cuenca have large historic sections. (so)

> *Quito has a large historic section, and so does Cuenca.*

1 Both Bangkok and São Paulo face many problems caused by too much traffic. (so)

2 Both Beijing and London have hosted the Olympic Games in the past. (too)

3 Vancouver and Taipei don't ever get very cold. (neither)

4 Seoul and Jakarta won't experience a decrease in their populations any time soon. (not either)

5 Both Hong Kong and Rio de Janeiro are famous for their physical beauty. (so)

6 Prague and Krakow attract people who like old historic architecture. (too)

7 The Prado Museum in Madrid and the Louvre in Paris shouldn't be missed. (neither)

8 Tokyo and Mexico City haven't lost their places among the world's largest cities yet. (not either)

So, too, neither, or not either: short responses

Use <u>so</u>, <u>too</u>, <u>neither</u>, or <u>not either</u> in short responses to express agreement.

A: I hate littering.
B: So do I. OR I do, **too**.
    NOT So do I ~~hate~~. / I do ~~hate~~, too.

A: I can't stand smoking.
B: I can't **either**. OR **Neither** can I.
    NOT I can't ~~stand~~ either. / Neither can I ~~stand~~.

It is common to express agreement with <u>Me, too</u> or <u>Me neither</u>.

A: I hate littering.
B: Me, too.

A: I can't stand smoking.
B: Me neither.

C Agree with each statement three ways, using short responses with <u>so</u>, <u>too</u>, <u>neither</u>, or <u>(not) either</u>.

1 "I've never been to Ulan Bator."
You: ....

2 "I can't figure this out."
You: ....

3 "I loved going there!"
You: ....

4 "I have to get some cash."
You: ....

5 "I'm getting really tired."
You: ....

6 "I used to travel more."
You: ....

7 "I'll call her tomorrow."
You: ....

8 "I'm not going to tell her she's late."
You: ....

Pronunciation Booster

The Pronunciation Booster is optional. It provides a pronunciation lesson and practice to support speaking in each unit, making students' speech more comprehensible.

UNIT 1

Content words and function words

In English, content words are generally stressed.
Function words are generally unstressed.

My **BOSS** is a **PAIN** in the **NECK**!
He's **REALLY** a **TERRIFIC BOSS**.
MARK is **SUCH** a **SMART GUY**.
I'm **SURE** she'll be a **GREAT MANAGER**.

Stress in compound nouns

Many compound nouns are made up of two nouns, with the first one modifying the second one. In these compounds, stress usually falls on the first noun. However when a noun is modified by an adjective, stress is equal on both words.

noun + noun		adjective + noun
I drink **APPLE** juice.	BUT	I like **RED APPLES**.
She's a **PEOPLE** person.	BUT	She's a **NICE PERSON**.
It's an **APARTMENT** building.	BUT	It's a **TALL BUILDING**.
They're **EXERCISE** machines.	BUT	They're **NEW MACHINES**.

Content words

nouns	boss, Julie, happiness
verbs	find, meet, call
adjectives	talkative, small, green
adverbs	quietly, again, very
possessive pronouns	mine, yours, his
demonstrative pronouns	this, those, that
reflexive pronouns	ourselves, herself
interrogative pronouns	what, who, where

Function words

prepositions	of, from, at
conjunctions	and, but, or
determiners	a, the, some
personal pronouns	he, she, they
possessive adjectives	my, her, their
auxiliary verbs	have + [past participle]
	be + [present participle]

Be careful! When an auxiliary verb is negative or used in short answers, it is generally stressed.

I **CAN'T GO**.	He **WON'T LIKE** it.
No, they **DON'T**.	Yes, I **HAVE**.

A ▶6:01 Listen and practice.

1 My **BOSS** is a **PAIN** in the **NECK**.
2 He's **REALLY** a **TERRIFIC BOSS**.
3 **MARK** is **SUCH** a **SMART GUY**.
4 I'm **SURE** she'll be a **GREAT MANAGER**.

B Circle the content words.

1 Learn to live in the present.
2 He reminded me to call my mother.
3 He asked me to work faster.
4 I prefer to stick closer to home.

▶6:02 Now practice reading each sentence aloud and listen to compare.* (Note that your choices may differ from what you hear on the audio.)

C ▶6:03 Listen and practice.

1 I drink **APPLE** juice. I like **RED APPLES**.
2 She's a **PEOPLE** person. She's a **NICE PERSON**.
3 It's an **APARTMENT** building. It's a **TALL BUILDING**.
4 They're **EXERCISE** machines. They're **NEW MACHINES**.

D ▶6:04 Practice reading each compound noun aloud and then listen to check.*

1 global warming
2 tennis courts
3 a reliable person
4 a telephone directory
5 office managers
6 the bullet train

*Note: Whenever you see a listening activity with an asterisk (*), say each word, phrase, or sentence in the pause after you hear each number. Then listen for confirmation.

Intonation patterns

In statements, commands, and information questions, lower pitch after the stressed syllable in the last stressed word. If the last syllable in the sentence is stressed, lower pitch on the vowel by lengthening it.

I haven't been going to many concerts lately.

Don't forget to watch them on YouTube tonight.

How long have you been listening to that song?

She's been practicing for several months.

Raise pitch after the stressed syllable in the last stressed word in <u>yes</u> / <u>no</u> questions and requests. If the last syllable in the sentence is stressed, raise pitch on the vowel by lengthening it.

Have you been listening to Christina Perri lately?

Could you pick up the tickets for me?

Do you think she has a nice voice?

Has he been checking online?

A ▶6:05 **Listen and practice.**

1 I haven't been going to many concerts lately.

2 Don't forget to watch them on YouTube tonight.

3 How long have you been listening to that song?

4 She's been practicing for several months.

5 Have you been listening to Christina Perri lately?

6 Could you pick up the tickets for me?

7 Do you think she has a nice voice?

8 Has he been checking online?

B Circle the last stressed content word in each of the following sentences. If that word has more than one syllable, underline the stressed syllable.

1 That song has a great beat you can dance to.

2 Her catchy lyrics make you want to sing along.

3 Didn't you like that song's melody?

4 What time do you think the concert will be finished?

5 How long has she been dancing to that song?

▶6:06 **Now practice reading each sentence aloud, using the intonation patterns you have learned. Listen to check.***

Sentence rhythm: thought groups

Examples of thought groups	
subject + verb	I don't know
noun phrases	my short-term goal
prepositional phrases	by the end of the month
predicates	is drowning in debt
noun clauses	where the money goes
adjective clauses	that I paid off last year
adverbial clauses	when I've finished my report

Longer sentences are usually divided by rhythm into smaller "thought groups"—groups of words that naturally or logically go together. Exactly how statements may be divided into thought groups will vary among speakers.

My short-term goal / is to start living / within my means.

NOT My short-term / goal is to / start living within my / means.

I don't plan / to be financially dependent / for the rest of my life.

By next year / I hope to have gotten / a good job / as a financial consultant.

Pitch in longer sentences

In longer sentences, pitch may fall—or rise—after the last stressed syllable in each thought group, with no change in meaning.

Once he tries keeping / a realistic budget / he'll find it easy / to save money. **OR**

Once he tries keeping / a realistic budget / he'll find it easy / to save money.

A ▶6:07 **Listen and practice.**

1 My short-term goal is to start living within my means.

2 I don't plan to be financially dependent for the rest of my life.

3 By next year, I hope to have gotten a good job as a financial consultant.

4 a Once he tries keeping a realistic budget, he'll find it easy to save money.

4 b Once he tries keeping a realistic budget, he'll find it easy to save money.

B **Read the following sentences. Decide how you might break each sentence into thought groups.**

1 By the end of this month, I hope to have finished paying off my student loans.

2 In two months, when we've finally paid off our house, we're going to have a big party to celebrate.

3 To be perfectly honest, I couldn't tell you where the money goes.

4 By next year, I will have completed my studies, but I don't think I will have gotten married.

DIGITAL
PAIR
WORK

▶6:08 **Now practice reading each sentence aloud, paying attention to pitch. Listen to compare.*** (Note that your choices may differ from what you hear on the audio.)

UNIT 4

Linking sounds

Linking with vowels

When the final consonant sound of a word is followed by a vowel sound, link the sounds together.

It's_in style now.

She bought him_an_elegant tie.

I've_already bought_a new suit.

Linking identical consonants

When the final consonant sound of a word is followed by the same sound, link the sounds together as one sound.

The blouse is_striped.

They preferred_dark suits.

What an attractive_vest!

A ► 6:09 **Listen and practice.**

1 It's in style now.

2 She bought him an elegant tie.

3 I've already bought a new suit.

4 The blouse is striped.

5 They preferred dark suits.

6 What an attractive vest!

B **Underline all the places where you think the sounds should be linked.**

1 She wants Susan to dress up next time.

2 It's fashionable and elegant.

3 It's out of style.

4 I wish she preferred dressing down.

5 That blouse isn't trendy enough for my taste.

6 I think Kyle has stylish taste.

 ► 6:10 **Now practice reading each sentence aloud and listen to check.***

UNIT 5

Unstressed syllables: vowel reduction to /ə/

In conversation, the vowels in unstressed syllables are often reduced to the sound /ə/. The vowel sound /ə/ occurs more often in English than any other vowel sound and contributes to maintaining the rhythm of English.

· — · ·			· · — · ·		
ac cept a ble	→	/ək'septəbəl/	ir re spon si ble	→	/ˌɪrə'spɑnsəbəl/
· — · ·			· —		
con sid er ate	→	/kən'sɪdərət/	po lite	→	/pə'laɪt/
· · — · ·			· — ·		
dis o be di ent	→	/ˌdɪsə'bidiənt/	re spect ful	→	/rə'spektfəl/
· · — · ·			· — ·		
in ex cus a ble	→	/ˌɪnək'skyuzəbəl/	ri dic u lous	→	/rɪ'dɪkyələs/

A ► 6:11 **Listen and practice.**

1 acceptable

2 considerate

3 disobedient

4 inexcusable

5 irresponsible

6 polite

7 respectful

8 ridiculous

B ► 6:12 **Listen to each word and circle the unstressed syllables that have the sound /ə/.**

1 un ac cept a ble

2 in con si de rate

3 im po lite

4 un pleas ant

5 ir ra tion al

6 im ma ture

7 un i mag i na ble

8 dis re spect ful

9 in ap pro pri ate

► 6:13 **Now practice reading each word aloud and listen again to check.***

Test-Taking Skills Booster

The Test-Taking Skills Booster is optional. It provides practice in applying some key logical thinking and comprehension skills typically included in reading and listening tasks on standardized proficiency tests. Each unit contains one Reading Completion activity and one or more Listening Completion activities.

The reading selections in the Booster are either adaptations of those from the *Summit 1* units or new reading selections about a related topic. Listening Completion exercises are based on the listening passages that can be found on the audio from the *Summit* units. None of the Reading Completion or Listening Completion tasks duplicate what students have already done in the unit.

*Note that the practice activities in the Booster are not intended to test student achievement after each unit. Complete Achievement Tests for *Summit* can be found in the *Summit* ActiveTeach.

READING COMPLETION
Read the selection. Choose the word or phrase that best completes each statement.

The Lost Ring

Last weekend, ... she was shopping for a new car, Laura Mills found a ring on the floor of one of
$\overline{1}$
the cars she was test-driving. She picked it up and put it in her purse, intending to ask the car salesman if a

customer had .... a lost ring. However, by the time she arrived back at the car dealership, she had
$\overline{2}$
forgotten about the ring and headed toward home, thinking about .... she should buy one of the cars
$\overline{3}$
she had test-driven. Once home, she opened her purse to put in her keys and discovered the ring. "I felt sort

of like a thief, but I certainly hadn't .... to steal the ring. I wondered what I should do."
$\overline{4}$

.... driving back to the car dealership immediately, she took the time to examine the ring for any
$\overline{5}$
identifying information and found this inscription engraved inside: *To my love on our marriage. BT to LS 2005.*

In a burst of creative thinking, Mills thought one of her friends might .... the ring, so she posted the
$\overline{6}$
photo of it on Facebook but was .... not to show the inscription. She urged her friends to share it, with
$\overline{7}$
this message: "Have you lost this ring? I found it at Spotless Car Dealership on the floor of a car. .... it
$\overline{8}$
is yours, identify it with the information on the inscription inside." To her surprise, she got a message from the

owner just two hours later.

1 **A** except	**B** while	**C** during	**D** because
2 **A** reported	**B** said	**C** wanted	**D** stolen
3 **A** since	**B** no matter	**C** whether	**D** after
4 **A** meant	**B** decided	**C** believed	**D** included
5 **A** Because of	**B** In spite of	**C** Rather than	**D** Due to
6 **A** relate	**B** recognize	**C** resemble	**D** resurrect
7 **A** afraid	**B** satisfied	**C** needless	**D** careful
8 **A** Whether	**B** No matter	**C** Suppose	**D** If

LISTENING COMPLETION

▶ 6:32 You will hear a conversation. Read the paragraph below. Then listen and complete each statement with the word or short phrase you hear in the conversation. Listen a second time to check your work.

The woman thinks that crime is out of (1) .... She says that the (2) .... is full of crime stories. The man agrees, and he thinks crime represents the whole breakdown in (3) .... The woman feels hopeless about the situation, but the man thinks there's something we can (4) .... about crime. First, he says the local (5) .... need more money to fight crime. His second suggestion is not to (6) .... a lot of jewelry on the street.

UNIT 2

READING COMPLETION
Read the selection. Choose the word or phrase that best completes each statement.

Ludwig van Beethoven

The gifted young Ludwig van Beethoven had already composed his first piece of music by the time he was twelve. .... , at the age of sixteen, he went to study in Vienna, Austria, the .... of European

1   **2**

cultural life at the time and home to the most brilliant musicians and composers of the period. Beethoven proved to be an imaginative composer.

.... Beethoven remembered for his great genius, but also for his strong and difficult personality.

3

In one infamous incident, Beethoven became so annoyed with a waiter that he behaved rudely, emptying a plate of food over the man's head. .... , he could be quite egotistical, saying once, "There are and will

4

be thousands of princes. There is only one Beethoven." .... anyone in the audience talked during a

5

concert, he would stop immediately and walk out. Many in musical and aristocratic circles admired Beethoven .... his difficult behavior, and they knew he might lose his .... at any time. They always forgave

6   **7**

his insults and moody temperament. Beethoven was also well-known for his .... and eccentric

8

behavior. He often walked through the streets of Vienna muttering to himself, and he completely neglected his personal appearance. Because he would always let his clothes get dirty, his friends would .... during

9

the night and replace them with new ones.

1	**A** Likewise	**B** Then	**C** Since	**D** Now that
2	**A** heart	**B** importance	**C** well-known	**D** beginning
3	**A** Neither is	**B** Even if	**C** Not only is	**D** However
4	**A** In contrast	**B** In addition	**C** While	**D** As a result
5	**A** For instance	**B** While	**C** If	**D** Because
6	**A** despite	**B** during	**C** even so	**D** even if
7	**A** music	**B** mind	**C** temper	**D** personality
8	**A** charming	**B** strange	**C** amusing	**D** likeable
9	**A** visit	**B** relax	**C** worry	**D** leave

LISTENING COMPLETION

A ▶6:33 You will hear a conversation. Read the paragraph below. Then listen and complete each statement with the word or short phrase you hear in the conversation. Listen a second time to check your work.

The man mentions that the actor Anthony Hopkins also (1) .... The woman is surprised and wants to know if the man has actually (2) .... the actor's music before. He says that he watched a video on (3) .... in which an (4) .... played one of his pieces. However, he found the music a little (5) .... for his taste.

B ▶6:34 You will hear a conversation. Read the paragraph below. Then listen and complete each statement with the word or short phrase you hear in the conversation. Listen a second time to check your work.

The woman wonders if the man likes (6) .... music and he says he's (7) .... it because it always makes him (8) .... However, she finds it (9) .... listen to because she thinks it always has the same (10) .... and every song (11) .... Whenever she hears it, she wants to (12) .... and listen to something else.

READING COMPLETION

Read the selection. Choose the word or phrase that best completes each statement.

Charitable Giving

Before deciding to .... money to a charity, it's important to look into the charity to be sure it's not a
fraud. .... we don't like to think that charitable organizations might be dishonest or take advantage of
2
our generosity, some charities—even ones with honest-sounding names—are not on the level.

Charities use the phone, face-to-face contact, e-mail, social networking sites, and mobile devices both
to solicit and .... donations. Scammers use the same methods to take advantage of your goodwill.
3
.... of how they reach you, you should .... any charity that refuses to .... detailed
4   **5**   **6**
information about its identity or how your money will be used. Be especially careful of a charity that uses a
name that closely resembles that of a better-known, ... organization. Another red flag is using high-
7
pressure tactics like trying to get you to donate immediately without giving you time to think about it or do
research. Be .... of charities that spring up too suddenly in response to current events and natural
8
disasters. .... they are legitimate, they probably don't have the infrastructure to get the donations
9
to the affected area or people. .... all the potential pitfalls, don't .... to donate to legitimate
10   **11**
charities. Charitable donations are one way of expressing your care for others and the environment.

1	**A** accept	**B** receive	**C** donate	**D** pay
2	**A** Because	**B** Although	**C** Nevertheless	**D** Since
3	**A** ask for	**B** return	**C** spend	**D** accept
4	**A** Because	**B** Regardless	**C** Since	**D** Otherwise
5	**A** avoid	**B** donate to	**C** select	**D** choose
6	**A** hide	**B** provide	**C** donate	**D** invest
7	**A** dishonest	**B** not on the level	**C** reputable	**D** illegal
8	**A** trusting	**B** wary	**C** shameful	**D** satisfied
9	**A** Even if	**B** Especially if	**C** Whether	**D** Because
10	**A** Although	**B** In spite of	**C** In case	**D** Similar to
11	**A** stop	**B** think	**C** hesitate	**D** remember

LISTENING COMPLETION

A ▶6:35 You will hear a conversation. Read the paragraph below. Then listen and complete each statement
with the word or short phrase you hear in the conversation. Listen a second time to check your work.

The man is asking the woman if she wants (1) .... for dinner. At first, she declines because she's
trying (2) .... But he insists, saying that he just got a big raise, and he suggests that they (3) ....
Again, she says no because she doesn't (4) .... right now, but the man offers to (5) ....

B ▶6:36 You will hear a conversation. Read the paragraph below. Then listen and complete each statement
with the word or short phrase you hear in the conversation. Listen a second time to check your work.

A man is visiting a woman and admiring her (6) .... furniture. He thinks the sofa is
(7) .... He imagines that it must have been (8) .... and asks her how she managed to pay
for it. She says that she (9) .... , putting away (10) ....very month. The man is envious and
wishes he could do the same thing. He feels bad because all his money is gone by (11) .... In spite of
the fact that he makes (12) .... , he just doesn't know where all (13) .... goes.

READING COMPLETION

Read the selection. Choose the word or phrase that best completes each statement.

The Media and Women's Self-esteem

It has been reported that 75 percent of women in the United States think they are "too fat." What is the cause of this? .... some people, media such as television, movies, and magazines actually define a woman's "beauty" for us by providing images that represent the ideal. .... the ideal today is tall and thin, women want to be tall and thin, too, ... for the majority, this goal is unattainable. .... hair color or weight, which are somewhat under our control, height and body type are largely determined by genetics and .... are not controllable. .... , since the average fashion model is 5 feet, 11 inches (1.83 meters) tall and weighs 117 pounds (53 kilograms), ... the average woman is only 5 feet, 4 inches (1.65 meters) tall and weighs approximately 140 pounds (63.5 kilograms), very few women could fall into the "ideal" range. .... , many women are left feeling either fat or unattractive.

Perhaps more important is the fact that constantly viewing images of models and actresses causes even very young girls to grow up with a negative self-image and .... self-esteem. .... it would be impractical to try to change the images being presented in the media, we can make an effort to help young people understand that they are being targeted as a consumer group so advertisers can convince them to buy products.

1	**A** Because	**B** As a consequence of	**C** According to	**D** Therefore
2	**A** Due to the fact that	**B** As a result	**C** Although	**D** Consequently
3	**A** because	**B** even though	**C** as a consequence	**D** likewise
4	**A** Unlike	**B** Like	**C** In similar fashion	**D** Whereas
5	**A** not either	**B** therefore	**C** however	**D** as well
6	**A** Because	**B** In contrast	**C** Furthermore	**D** Although
7	**A** whereas	**B** even though	**C** similarly	**D** unlike
8	**A** However	**B** In contrast	**C** For instance	**D** As a result
9	**A** excellent	**B** high	**C** happy	**D** low
10	**A** Although	**B** Following that	**C** Before	**D** After that

LISTENING COMPLETION

A ▶6:37 You will hear a conversation. Read the paragraph below. Then listen and complete each statement with the word or short phrase you hear in the conversation. Listen a second time to check your work.

The first woman is looking at a (1) .... and would like the other woman's opinion of it. She is thinking of wearing it for her presentation at the (2) .... She asks the other woman if it might be (3) .... The second woman thinks the dress might be better on a younger woman. She thinks clothes for women their age should be more (4) ....

B ▶6:38 You will hear a conversation. Read the paragraph below. Then listen and complete each statement with the word or short phrase you hear in the conversation. Listen a second time to check your work.

The customer is shopping for a shirt for (5) .... He's thinking he'd like something in a (6) .... color, perhaps in a (7) .... or green. The salesman asks whether the customer is looking for a (8) .... or a (9) .... shirt. The customer says that he'd like a long-sleeve one, and the clerk offers to show him some (10) .... ones for him (11) .... from.

READING COMPLETION

Read the selection. Choose the word or phrase that best completes each statement.

Avoiding Urban Crime

.... the 21st century, there has been a steady increase in the number of foreign visitors to the great
1
cities of the world. Unfortunately, ... tourists to those places are particularly vulnerable to criminal
2
activities. Yet, there are precautions you can take to .... that you don't become a crime victim.
3

To begin with, avoid going out alone if .... There's usually safety in numbers, but don't
4
.... that tourist attractions also attract thieves. Stay aware of what's happening around you—as if you
5
had eyes in the back of your head. On the street, ... using a smartphone or tablet nor fumbling with a
6
map or guidebook is a good idea—unless of course you need to. Be particularly careful in crowds at festivals
or on buses and trains. And a warning to women: be careful if you carry a cross-body purse. Although wearing
one may .... it harder for a criminal to grab it from you, you could be injured if the purse-snatcher is on
7
a motorcycle.

At the hotel, ... leaving valuables unprotected in your room, where a burglar might break in and
8
take them. Ask the front desk to keep them for you. Better safe than sorry! Keep in mind that, all in all, crime
rates are going down worldwide, and the chances you will become a crime victim are low. So don't let
worrying about crime .... you from having a great time!
9

1	**A** Since	**B** In	**C** Now that	**D** As a result of
2	**A** part-time	**B** resident	**C** foreign	**D** friendly
3	**A** ensure	**B** avoid	**C** know	**D** attract
4	**A** unfamiliar	**B** expensive	**C** possible	**D** afraid
5	**A** remember	**B** forget	**C** realize	**D** worry
6	**A** not only	**B** neither	**C** either	**D** both
7	**A** make	**B** ensure	**C** take	**D** require
8	**A** remember	**B** forget	**C** avoid	**D** never
9	**A** confuse	**B** interfere	**C** encourage	**D** keep

LISTENING COMPLETION

▶ 6:39 **You will hear part of a report. Read the paragraph below. Then listen and complete each statement
with the word or short phrase you hear in the report. Listen a second time to check your work.**

Pete Frates was diagnosed with a rare disease called ALS that (1) .... the nervous system. He
came up with a big idea in order to (2) .... awareness of this terrible disease and to encourage people to
(3) .... to finding a cure. All people had to do was (4) .... in which they dump a bucket of icy
water over their heads and challenge (5) .... to either do the same or donate a hundred dollars. In social
media, people all over the world posted videos of (6) .... On Facebook, these videos were viewed
(7) .... times. Everyone (8) .... about the Ice Bucket Challenge. Even famous
(9) .... and (10) .... were taking the challenge and posting videos.